I Was Sick and You Visited Me

I WAS SICK AND YOU VISITED ME

A Spiritual Guide for Catholics in Hospital Ministry

Fernando Poyatos

PAULIST PRESS
New York/Mahwah, N.J.

Scriptural quotations are taken from: *The New American Bible* (Word, 1970, 1986, 1991), *The New King James Version* (Thomas Nelson, 1983), *Revised Standard Version* (Catholic Truth Society, 1966).

Cover design by Jim Brisson

Library of Congress Cataloging-in-Publication Data

Poyatos, Fernando.
    I was sick and you visited me : a spiritual guide for Catholics in hospital ministry / Fernando Poyatos.
        p.   cm.
    Includes bibliographical references and indexes.
    ISBN 0-8091-3871-9 (alk. paper)
    1. Church work with the sick. 2. Pastoral medicine—Catholic Church. I. Title.
BX2347.8.S5P68   1999
259´.4´08822—dc21   99-14352
                                                                          CIP

Published by Paulist Press
997 Macarthur Boulevard
Mahwah, New Jersey 07430

www.paulistpress.com

Printed and bound in the
United States of America

Contents

Contents

To those who allowed me to minister
to them in their suffering
and grow through them.

And to George Caldwell, a very special person who was included
on my Catholic patient list by mistake—although he hadn't
even been baptized in his own church—and became
not only one of my dearest friends,
but a fellow Catholic.

"Blessed be the God and Father of our Lord
Jesus Christ, the Father of compassion
and God of all encouragement, who encourages
us in our every affliction, so that we may be
able to encourage those who are in any affliction"
(*2 Corinthians 1:3–4*, NAB)

"Honor the physician with the honor due him
...for the Lord created him...pray to
the Lord, and He will heal you...
And give the physician his place..."
(*Sirach 38:1, 9, 12*, RSV)

"Those who visit the sick *must* be conveyors of
hope. When one has Jesus Christ's life in him,
he can see hope even in the most impossible
situations. God is a God of the impossible"
(Dr. Wm. S. Reed, *Healing the Whole Man:
Mind, Body, Spirit*, 138)

"Sickness may be the solemn occasion of
God's intervention in a person's life"
(Dr. Paul Tournier, *The Healing of Persons*, 198)

"We begin by imagining that we are giving to them;
we end by realizing that they have enriched us"
(*Pope John Paul II's homily in London, 1982*)

Preface

This book, designed as a spiritual manual for pastoral care workers, offers abundant material for seminars, workshops, and retreats, beyond pastoral care itself. Besides those gatherings designed to prepare new pastoral care visitors, individual topics could be presented at regular team meetings, followed by the participants' sharing of their experiences in that particular area.

Readers will find that, despite occasional references to specific Roman Catholic issues, the book transcends denominational barriers, in the spirit of ecumenism and of growing mutual awareness and love which God always willed for his children.

I wish to thank Rev. Lawrence Boadt, Paulist Press, and his editors for their valuable advice and suggestions.

Above all, I must express my gratitude to all the Catholic and non-Catholic patients with whom I have interacted at the Dr. Everett Chalmers Hospital in Fredericton, New Brunswick, Canada. Most returned to their homes, others "have fallen asleep," as Paul would put it, but they all remain deep in my heart.

Fredericton, Canada
All Saints Day, 1997

1

Chapter 1 ·
The Sick, Brothers and Sisters in Christ, and Us

May the God of peace himself make you perfectly holy and may you entirely, spirit, soul, and body, be preserved blameless for the coming of our Lord Jesus Christ (1 Thes 5:23, NAB)

1. The importance of pastoral care: Samaritans and harvesters in God's kingdom

I had a very special feeling the first day I went to the Pastoral Care Office of the Everett Chalmers Hospital, in Fredericton, New Brunswick, Canada. I had been recommended by my pastor and accepted by the person in charge of the Roman Catholic team and the supervising priest. It was a busy place at times, with a flurry of ministers and lay volunteers like me signing the register book, getting their patient lists from the computer, and starting out for the different floors. Although I had visited hospitals many times, that day I was overwhelmed by the realization that I was in a unique enclosure where part of society had to deal with its suffering, and

3

faced expectation, uncertainty, or crisis, even in bringing new life to the world. Seeing myself as part of the so-called healthy majority, it suddenly dawned on me with gratitude that God had given me the opportunity to carry out what is the duty of that majority: to serve the other part, the sick and the suffering. As I stepped into the rooms that day and met the eyes of my first patients, I understood deeply the social and spiritual importance of pastoral care and the great need those brothers and sisters had for a relationship with us.

Two things became clear to me that first day. First, the sick have a moral right to not be alone, but to relate to others while they suffer, even more than when they do not. I looked at the stream of visitors during visiting hours. As they stepped out into the street, I could sense from experience their instinctive satisfaction at being among the fortunate upon whom the sun cast its warm rays as they left behind suffering and even death. But now, having been given the privilege of joining pastoral care, I also became aware of its immense relevance in society both for the sick and for all who look after them, completing the care of the whole human being: body, mind, and spirit. I realized that God puts in our hearts the desire to engage in this ministry. We are allowed through his goodness not only to become his Samaritans, but also "ambassadors for Christ" (2 Cor 5:20, NAB), God's harvesters in the vast field of his suffering children. "The harvest truly is great, but the laborers are few" (Lk 10:2, NKJ).

For anyone in hospital or home pastoral care visitation, whether clergy, religious, or lay, this ministry soon becomes a daily discovery of their spiritual state as God's children and as members of the Body of Christ. As a Roman Catholic lay visitor and Eucharistic minister, always in close contact with non-Catholics, I realized from the beginning that this ministry was based on Jesus' words, "I was sick and you visited me." I further realized that, as Christians, we should approach it *only* from a Christian perspective and with a Christian attitude. Every situation and problem encountered, independent of

4

our religious denomination, has its comment or answer in scripture, the unfailing beacon for us all.[1] In our multiple sufferings of body, mind and spirit, we confront crucial problems. As our hearts attune to those of our brothers and sisters, we strive to help those in our care. In the process they help us to grow spiritually through our need, in this modern, materialistic world, for evangelization, Christian counseling, prayer, the Bible, and, within the Catholic Church, for the sacraments of reconciliation and communion.

2. Receiving when giving: Growth through pastoral care ministry

As time in this ministry goes by, we realize that, as Pope John Paul II said, "We begin by imagining that we are giving to them; we end by realizing that they have enriched us." It is in this frequent confrontation with the suffering of so many brothers and sisters, in their sharing of their emotional and spiritual journeys, and at times even in their quiet rejection of us, that they become a strong support in our own journey and an instrument of spiritual growth. Thus, although it is true that, as Jesus said, "it is more blessed to give than to receive" (Acts 20:35, NAB), patients and visitors are a blessing to each other and the caregiver can profit much in every instance, regardless of the situation. Once, as I was praying for a retired Air Force officer who was undergoing chemotherapy, I felt his hand stroking my shoulder with a brotherly touch, perhaps because I had told him that I had been a little down lately and asked for his prayers. It was a great boost. Often those with whom I pray assure me that they are also praying for me.

3. "You are not far from the kingdom of God"

Jesus' words in Mark 12:34, addressed to the scribe who had professed his love for God and neighbor, come to mind in the context of pastoral care. Our hospital ministry, done out of love for God and others, will definitely bring us closer to God. Jesus was also quoting the Law (Dt 6:5) and said to the scribe who asked him which was the first of all the commandments:

> "You shall love the Lord your God with all your heart, with all your soul, with all your mind, and with all your strength...." And the second, like it, is this: "You shall love your neighbor as yourself." There is no other commandment greater than these (Mk 12:30-31, NKJ).

Besides our own pondering of those key words, "heart," "soul," "mind," "strength," St. Augustine tells us:

> Love of God is the first love commanded, love of neighbor the first love exercised.... it is by loving your neighbor that you shall come some day to see your God. By loving your neighbor you purify the eyes that shall see God, as John indicates when he says: "If you do not love your neighbor whom you see, how can you love God whom you do not see?"

Lest we have any doubts about where to get this kind of love for our patients, St. Augustine responds: "from God, the one who gives you the power to love."[2] Let us ask Jesus for that love, for he is continually interceding for us and he will give it to us (Heb 7:25). Since we all need encouragement, let us always remember Jesus' last words to that scribe: "You are not far from the kingdom of God" (Mk 12:34, NAB).

4. Pastoral care and the pursuit of holiness

"Sanctify yourselves, then, and be holy; for I, the Lord, your God, am holy" (Lv 20:7, NAB). As Christians, we know that holiness depends on our everyday life, not on "great deeds of holiness." Thus, we must pray to God that our pastoral healthcare work be a natural, Spirit-led pursuit of holiness. Without the Spirit's help, we run the risk of pursuing our self-image, good feelings about being good and doing good, or a sense of spiritual accomplishment. Let us remember that what God wants is "mercy and not sacrifice" (Hos 6:6, NKJ; Mt 9:13, NKJ). For him the true proof of holiness lies in what we do for others. It is in how we carry out our duties, with a heart filled with love for the patients, "for whoever does not love a brother whom he has seen cannot love God whom he has not seen" (1 Jn 4:20, NAB).

It is by our relationship with people, specifically with our patients in pastoral care, that we will be able to measure our relationship with God and see how authentic our pursuit of holiness is. This has nothing to do with "feeling holy"; we cannot measure our holiness by how we feel. Rather, it is a question of "relating to others in a holy way," gently guided by the Holy Spirit, for St. Paul tells us, "Pursue peace with all men, and holiness, without which no one will see the Lord" (Heb 12:14, NKJ). On the other hand, we may feel unworthy, but God, not ourselves, has put us there. I must struggle now and then, trying not to fall into this trap.

5. Suffering: Coping with our oldest mystery

"If the angels were capable of envy, they would envy us for two things; one is the receiving of Holy Communion, and the other is suffering,"[3] wrote recently beatified Sr. Faustina Kowalska (d. 1938), one of the many holy persons mysteriously chosen by God for suffering, or who offered their suffering to him.[4] Although Chapter 6 will address the issue of suffering at some length, we must recognize now that, if we care to look, wherever we go we are confronted with suffering, not always physical suffering but, at deeper levels, the ongoing pain of life's hurts that invade one's whole being with greater force when weakened by sickness. We realize that if we identify with the sick as we ought, if we see Jesus in each one of them and strive to minister to them in his name, we discover that we must know how to deal with that suffering on their behalf. As witnesses of Jesus, we have a mandate to inspire in them, by the way we speak and pray with them, the conviction that "suffering, a consequence of original sin, acquires a new meaning; it becomes a participation in the saving work of Jesus" (*Catechism of the Catholic Church,* #1521).[5] To our brothers and sisters who suffer, we must be the light of God that will help them hear God saying that to them.

As we confront suffering, we confront something else as well. We see patients who suddenly wonder why there is evil in the world, why there is suffering, and why they are suffering if they have not done anything really bad, while bad people live happily. How hard those questions and statements hit us. We could say that suffering *is* suffering precisely because, or *when,* we see no reason for it. If we try to be "logical," "Suffering, injustice and death, seem to contradict the Good News, they can shake our faith and become a temptation against us," as John Paul II wrote in his 1984 encyclical, *Salvifici Doloris.*

> The sense of the uselessness of suffering...sometimes very strongly rooted in human suffering...not only consumes the person interiorly, but seems to make him a burden to others...condemned to receive help and assistance from others (#27).

Those "others" includes pastoral care visitors who want to help, and we see this many times as we visit; that is why it is so much "easier" to visit with a person of firm faith, even a terminal patient, who ministers to us by strengthening our own faith. How can we help many others who, once they are struck with illness, remain alone in their suffering, alone because they are not *with* Jesus, although Jesus is with them? John Paul II has also said that part of our mission of evangelization to the sick is "trying to enlighten, by communicating the evangelical values, the way of living, suffering and dying of the men in our time" ("Care of the Sick"). In a 1984 homily to several hundred sick people, he encouraged them by saying:

Dear sick! Offer your sufferings to the Lord with love and with generosity for the conversion of the world! Man must understand the gravity of sin, of offending God, and be converted to him who, through love, created him and calls him to everlasting happiness.... Accept your pains with courage and confidence, also for those who are suffering in the world.... The Church needs people who pray and love in silence and in suffering: and in your infirmity, you can truly be these apostles!

And for the 1997 Day of the Sick, John Paul said:

Suffering and illness belong to the human condition. However, in the death and resurrection of Christ, humanity discovers a new dimension of its suffering; instead of a failure, it reveals itself as an occasion for offering a testimony of faith and of love.

Not too many of us truly believe that "all things work for good for those who love God" (Rom 8:28, NAB), but are we quite ready to apply those words at the dentist's when we expect and endure pain there? How many of us, as our first reaction to suffering or impending suffering, believe that we are about to take Christ's cross upon our shoulders? How many of us, who want to be good Christians, truly believe in Jesus' own warnings about suffering, when he tells us that following him is not easy: "How narrow the gate and constricted the road that leads to life" (Mt 7:14, NAB). Suffering is not just physical; it can be caused by a friend's ingratitude, or by an unbelieving or unfaithful spouse. It is terrible to suffer when, besides confronting us with death, it seems pointless, when we cannot see any meaning in it, when we lack faith to accept the gift of Christ's suffering for us on the cross. Do we really believe that "God so loved the world that he gave his only begotten Son, that whoever believes in him should not perish but have everlasting life" (Jn 3:16, NKJ), and that he gave him, himself made man, through a most painful and humiliating death?

6. "Our struggle is not with flesh and blood"

Thus, we see that since we are body, mind, and spirit, suffering physically or psychologically debilitates body, mind, and also spirit when we are caught without "the whole armor of God" (Eph 6:11, NKJ) of strong faith and hope. Sickness is not life but death, not light but darkness. We must admit, without fearing them, that too many "unclean spirits" (Mk 1:27, NAB) like those cast out by Jesus in his ministry may be attacking patients and may have taken abode in them. Sometimes that is what pastoral workers confront in a hospital or a home: "There was a woman who had a spirit of infirmity eighteen years" (Lk 13:11, NKJ). This is not to say that we should bring this up or even mention it while visiting and praying with the patients. But we must acknowledge the specific presence of evil, for we know that "we do not wrestle against flesh and blood, but against...spiritual hosts" (Eph 6:12, NKJ).

Trying to play the role of Job's well-meaning friends by suggesting that sickness is the consequence of the person's sin can do much harm. While not dismissing the possibility, we must not jump to conclusions regarding anyone. Instead, let us remember that Jesus told those who asked him about the man born blind that "neither he nor his parents sinned" (Jn 9:2, NAB), and affirmed that those poor Galileans who were caught under a collapsed tower were not worse sinners than others (Lk 13:2–3).

We must be extremely careful to avoid making any connection between sickness and sin unless the patient brings it up. Nevertheless, it is necessary to be clearly aware, without fanaticism, of the possibility of the relationship between personal sin and suffering, the consequences of the sin in our family tree,[6] and the relationship between the sin of the world and collective and individual suffering, without interpreting suffering as a direct punishment from God. It is essential to be aware—and knowledge of scripture is indispensable here—of the often-unsuspected relationship between God's love and suffering as well as of the value of suffering that God may allow. Both the Old and New Testaments eloquently teach us about and illustrate these relationships. Familiarity with the divine teachings on these subjects will greatly help in pastoral care.

7. Caring for the whole person: Body-mind-spirit

At the same time, to be aware of those relationships, we need to acknowledge that a person is an indivisible unit in which body, mind, and spirit are not separate but interrelated parts. God "created man in his image, in the divine image [God's spiritual nature]" (Gn 1:27, NAB), but he did it "out of the clay of the ground" (Gn 2:7, NAB). He thus blended body, mind, and soul and created a being that was physical, but also like him who "is Spirit" (Jn 4:24, NAB). This is the form in which God, from eternity, chose to come to us, because he "so loved the world" (Jn 3:16, NKJ). This is what we face every time we approach another. We all experience how physical health can affect our spiritual well-being. Our state of mind can make our body sick, and a serious imbalance in our relationship with God can affect our physical and even mental state, just as keeping close to God positively affects our whole being. Let us comfort our suffering brothers and sisters by quoting, paraphrasing, or reading to them the psalmist's words:

> I keep the Lord always before me; with the Lord at my right,
> I shall never be shaken. Therefore my heart is glad, my soul
> rejoices, my body also dwells secure (Ps 16: 8-9, NAB).

We are called, therefore, within the limits of our role in pastoral care, to minister to the whole person, who may be as much in need of inner healing (so important among Christians today) as physical healing. This means being aware of their indivisible tripartite nature as God's creatures. Many truly Christian doctors such as those within Christian Medical Foundation International (CMFI) know this well and, combining their God-given medical knowledge with their spiritual knowledge, "will pray to the Lord" (Sir 38:14, RSV). Perhaps the words I utter most often in prayer with a patient are: "Lord, I ask you to fill his mind, heart, and body with your presence and your peace, which are already healing." Like the psalmist, Paul also acknowledges this triple reality of ours:

> Now may the God of peace himself sanctify you completely; and may your whole spirit, soul and body be preserved blameless (1 Thes 5:23, NKJ).

8. The pastoral care visitor, promoter of medicine and prayer

At the beginning of my lay ministry, a patient told me that a doctor had asked her, "Did he tell you God was going to heal you?" (that is, without medicines?). I never said that, of course, and none of the Christian doctors I met at Christian Medical Foundation would ask such a question. Its president, Dr. William Reed, quoted at their conference a favorite passage in the book of Sirach.[7] I wish all doctors were familiar with the Bible and with that book in which God tells us that sin can cause illness and that we should resort to both the physician and him who ultimately works through the former, particularly when the doctor is a true believer who sees himself as God's instrument:

> And he gave skill to men that he might be glorified in his marvelous works. By them he heals and takes away pain (Sir 38:6-7, RSV).

It does not seem to be an option for the physician to pray for his patients as do Christian Medical Foundation doctors and many others, when we are told,

And give the physician his place, for the Lord created him....
they too will pray to the Lord that he should grant them suc-
cess in diagnosis and in healing, for the sake of preserving
life (Sir 38:12, 14, RSV).

Thus, a patient is not only a body for the internist, or a mind for
the psychiatrist, nor a soul for us, but a whole, integrated being
become ill. How sad it is when we meet those who have been
rushed to the hospital, eager for the doctor, but when we offer to
pray say, "No, thank you, I'm all right." We can always pray
silently or elsewhere. And "whatever you do, in word or in deed,
do everything in the name of the Lord Jesus" (Col 3:17, NAB).

Chapter 2 ·
Relationship
and Evangelization

"Feed my lambs" (Jn 21:16, NKJ)

1. The sick, God, and us: Four principles

Pastoral care ministry should be based on four principles. The first principle is that patients are brothers and sisters in Christ, whom we must approach with love, responsibility, and reverence. *Love,* because of the very nature of the relationship we have acquired as children of God the Father through his Son Jesus Christ, as "heirs of God and joint heirs with Christ" (Rom 8:17, NAB). *Responsibility,* because we are not in pastoral care on our own initiative, but God's, who has placed us there as "ambassadors of Christ, as if God were pleading through us" (2 Cor 5:20, NAB). And *reverence,* because those brothers and sisters in God are his creatures, created "in his own image" (Gn 1:27, RSV). If Christian physicians like surgeon William Reed promote a much-needed "reverence for tissue," meaning for every tissue with which they come in contact in the operating room,[8] how much more must we relate to the whole person with reverence. We should refer to them as "my brother___" or "my sister___" when praying with them. This will establish an important bond at the onset of the visit.

The second principle goes even further. In the words of St. Paul, referring to when he was sick: "You did not scorn or despise me, but received me as an angel of God, as Jesus Christ" (Gal 4:14, RSV). This is how Mother Teresa's sisters see each person for whom they care, as she once told me in Calcutta. Neither Paul nor Mother Teresa exaggerate, for Jesus said: "Assuredly, I say to you, inasmuch as you did it to one of the least of these my brethren, you did it to me" (Mt 25:40, NKJ). I know as I enter a patient's room that Jesus loves him or her very much. It is by God's permissive will (because he allows it) or volitive will (because he wills it) that they find themselves helpless, unable to do anything, and vulnerable to depression, social and spiritual discouragement, fear, and other negative feelings. I know from my own experience that "whom the Lord loves he chastens" (Heb 12:6, NKJ). Above all, I know that "he bruises, but he binds up; he wounds, but his hands make whole" (Jb 5:18, NKJ).

The third principle is that while they are vulnerable to the enemy, Satan, they are also vulnerable and particularly open to God's grace. This is when the clergy and we come into their lives, just as the physician does. As ministers of Christ to the sick, we must hear his voice saying, "in their affliction they will diligently seek me" (Hos 5:15, NKJ). Since they may need a little encouragement from us, we must discern the degree to which we should help them to seek God through Jesus personally and tangibly during their stay in the hospital. In different ways, while not precisely quoting scripture, we can say to them, "Seek the Lord while he may be found. Call upon him while he is near" (Is 55:6, NKJ).

Finally, the fourth principle is quite simple: we are there as "servants of Christ and stewards of the mysteries of God" (1 Cor

4:1, NAB). We can never properly serve our brothers and sisters unless we put on "the mind of Christ" (1 Cor 2:16, NAB). Nor can we be his stewards among the sick or anywhere, unless God fills us with the grace to care for them and know how to draw them to him, showing them the love and compassion of Jesus. One morning I did not feel up to visiting. The first patient the Lord led me to was an elderly woman in Palliative Care whom I helped with her breakfast and prayed for, after which she said with a glowing face: "Oh, it's been like being with the Lord!" I explained, while I stroked her forehead, that if she felt that way it was not because of me but because I was there *with* the Lord's love, which he put in my heart for her. According to his word, when I visited her I was visiting the Lord himself.

2. "If you show partiality, you commit sin"

Sometimes for various reasons that lie deep in our human frailty and imperfection, it may not be so easy just to love the person. If we visit the same patients a few times, we establish priorities and have our favorites, although we know that God, perfect as he is, shows no partiality. "If you really fulfill the royal law according to the scripture, 'You shall love your neighbor as yourself,' you do well; but if you show partiality, you commit sin, and are convicted by the law as transgressors" (Jas 2:8–9, NKJ).

I once visited a woman in her late fifties who had a stroke. She was a pitiable sight, her tongue protruding through one side of her mouth, drooling, unable to speak, and hardly able to communicate at all. As I caressed her forehead, I felt in my heart the love of Jesus for her. I often remember the beautiful testimony of my friend Lynn, a registered nurse. She had to tend to an elderly woman whom the other nurses would avoid because she was so unpleasant in every sense. Lynn asked God to put in her heart the kind of love she needed to relate to her, and on her first visit they were holding hands and she was telling Lynn about her life. This teaches us that whatever we can give our patients is not ours but God's. There is nothing to boast in, unless we boast in God (Ps 44:8/9, NAB), "for it is God who works in you both to will and to do" (Phil 2:13, NKJ).

3. Pastoral care and evangelization

In December 1978, as I sat across from her at a small table in the little parlor of her motherhouse in Calcutta, Mother Teresa told me, "What I can do, you cannot do, and what you can do, I cannot do. What are you?" "I am a university professor," I said. Quick as always, she replied, "Then just radiate Christ as what you are." By "radiating" she obviously meant evangelizing. The Bible tells us in different ways that we should radiate the two life-giving forces of light and warmth. Jesus Christ himself said, "I am the light of the world" (Jn 8:12, NAB), "I came into the world as a light, so that everyone who believes in me might not remain in darkness" (Jn 12:46, NAB), and told us to become "children of the light" (Jn 12:36, NAB). If "in him was life, and the life was the light of men" (Jn 1:4, NKJ), because Jesus is "the true light which gives light to every man" (Jn 1:9, NKJ), we who have received that light have an obligation not to hide it, but to heed his command, "Let your light so shine before men" (Mt 5:16, NKJ).

I hasten to say that I never approach a new person in the hospital or at home with any preconceived purpose of "evangelizing," let alone "preaching." Far from it. By evangelizing I mean, first, an attitude of witnessing to the gospel and, above all, to the kind of love that only God puts in our hearts. But when Jesus said, "You shall be my witnesses...to the end of the earth" (Acts 1:8, RSV), and "Go into all the world and preach the gospel to every creature" (Mk 16:15, NKJ), he meant, and continues to mean, *whoever* is in need of him. Since a hospital, like any other place, is full of people who need him, he is also saying, "Don't forget the hospitals." That is what John Paul II means when he refers to "the vast field of health, which is so important for announcing and witnessing the gospel."[9] As he tells us in his 1996 encyclical *Vita Consecrata:*

> The Church reminds consecrated men and women that a part of their mission is to *evangelize the healthcare centers* in which they work, striving to spread the light of gospel values to the way of living, suffering and dying of the people of our day (#83).

After all, evangelization is the foremost mandate of our Church today for everybody, constantly emphasized by John Paul II: "Every Christian should be aware that he is a messenger and an apostle, a spreader of the faith." Elsewhere he writes,

> Because the lay faithful belong to Christ, Lord and King of the universe, they share in his kingly ministry and are called by him to spread the kingdom in history...to make a gift of themselves so as to serve...Jesus, who is himself present in all his brothers and sisters, above all in the very least.[10]

This means we are called to spread Christ's kingdom on earth, to spread the truth which is the foundation of his kingdom: "For this I was born and for this I came into the world, to testify to the truth" (John 18:37, NAB). Whether or not we are active in evangelization, the evil one never ceases to counter God's work through us, for as John Paul II says, "There is also present a powerful anti-evangelization which is well organized and has the means to vigorously oppose the gospel and evangelization."[11] This includes all areas of our social life, from the workplace to the media, from the university classroom to the disorienting books that proliferate as signs of our times. As if all that were not enough, "the scandal of conflict between Christians obscures the scandal of the cross, thus crippling the one mission of the one Christ," as we read in the 1994 "ECT Statement."[12]

In our own sector of responsibility among the sick, we know that "pastoral work" means the "work of shepherding," that shepherding means tending to and leading others on a given path, and that the clergy are the true, God-anointed shepherds of the Church. Therefore, lay pastoral caregivers are there—as a lay apostolate needed and encouraged in today's Church—to assist the priests in functions they can assume as responsible Christians. This must be done in a spirit of service, and service is the heartbeat of our love for Jesus. That is why, when Peter answered "Yes" to his question "Do you love me?" Jesus replied, "Feed my lambs" (John 21:16, NKJ). If we serve we are imitating Jesus, who said that he "did not come to be served but to serve and to give his life as a ransom for many" (Mt 20:28, RSV). In addition, we are more than just serving Jesus and working "for him." We are "ministering to him," as Mother Teresa and the Canadian Pentecostal pastor Mark Buntain did in Calcutta, because Jesus says he is in each of those patients: "I was sick and you visited me...inasmuch as you did to one of the least of these my brethren, you did it to me" (Mt 25:36, 40, NKJ). They are Jesus, whether they welcome or reject us. God, as part of his plan for them, has allowed the circumstance whereby they have ended up in a hospital bed. Let us think, as we engage in conversation with them, and as they begin to tell us about themselves, so often in that spontaneous and therapeutic sharing when they know we listen with our hearts, that their being there, confronting the reality of suffering from which they might cringe, may have been the only way their loving Father could draw them closer to him and to those who can help them in his name. We may be his only instruments at that particular time. Once in Intensive Care I prayed for a man who could still hear my prayer, and the next day he died. Had God wanted me there the first time? Twice I went to see a man who had declined my offer to visit because he had been away from the Church for years. Nevertheless he held my hand and expressed his appreciation for my prayer. Did not God send me to him?

As Christians in the workplace or any other environment, we

must be mindful that each of those persons to whom we come in contact is, like ourselves, on his or her way to eternity. Perhaps God is giving that person, through us, an opportunity to come closer to him. I find that mind-boggling, but also disquieting when I consider my personal responsibility. How can we in this kind of shepherding work among the sick remain unaware that any of God's sheep might be the lost one that must be brought back to the fold? While we would like to bring them a member of the clergy, this may require that we minister to them first. What can be done except to "dialogue in an evangelizing way" when someone shares that he cannot forgive a relative, or that she does not go to church because she has not gone in a long time? A new patient began to tell me she did not go to church because she did not like the priest. Putting my hand on my Bible, I said to her: "God's absolution of your sins in confession is just as good from a 'bad' priest as it is from a 'good' one." I knew the point had been driven home and that was evangelization.

While we should consider ourselves "ambassadors for Christ" (2 Cor 6:20, NAB) and ambassadors for our Church and our priests, it is true that in this type of work we are also companions to the physicians and ministers "of Jesus Christ...ministering the gospel of God" (Rom 15:16, NKJ). We might even include the words I deleted from that verse, "Gentiles," since often we are dealing with persons who live, act, and think like pagans, whether they have been baptized or not. When I first began my pastoral ministry I realized, as a Catholic, what a privilege it was to minister to many who had been "sacramentalized but not evangelized," in whom God had yet to make the longest trip, from their minds to their hearts, turning "religion" into "relation."

Thus, in the hospital, as in any other environment, we share the clergy's responsibility to bring people back to God and uplift them spiritually when their faith is debilitated by suffering. Some of our Catholic patients may not be ready to receive communion, but we can always offer to pray, particularly if we have identified their

spiritual need. How can we be sure that the prayer we say with
our brother or sister will not be "vital" for eternity, particularly
when we suspect or know that we were the only ones who prayed
with them before they died? Our prayer can be the proclamation
of God's kingdom, a way to preach it without "preaching," evangelization. For, as St. Paul says in 1 Corinthians 9:16 (NAB), "Woe to
me if I do not preach it!"

4. Problematic, argumentative patients

Sometimes patients who want nothing from you, although they
truly need prayer, at the same time will not let you leave without
speaking their minds. There are different types, but they are all victims of the confusion sown in us by Satan, our enemy. The source of
this is the traditional ignorance of people about their own Church.
Trying to help them can seem useless; their minds are made up
about certain issues, but we can always try, up to a point, out of love
and compassion. Naturally, if an educated, intellectual unbeliever
ever allows us to get near him, he will probably give us a rough time
(if we are naive enough to allow it), for he might even want to discuss the very existence of God. As I am not the apostle Paul, I identify with the linguist Kenneth Pike, who says, regarding discussing
God with what he calls the "non-theistic intellectual," "I have given
up trying to reach the intellectual by argument."[13] Jesus knew this
very well when he told his Father, "Although you have hidden these
things from the wise and the learned you have revealed them to the
childlike" (Mt 11:25, NAB). Throughout the Old Testament we see
the attitude of God toward the proud, telling them, "The pride of
your heart has deceived you" (Ob 3, NAB), and telling us not to
"respect the proud" (or "those who stray after falsehood," or "false
gods"). That is why God's word warns, "Let no one deceive you with
empty arguments" (Eph 5:6, NAB). Thus, although we must speak
kindly to them as strayed brothers and sisters, we should shorten
our visit (unless the Spirit is leading us in a very special way). We

should not allow ourselves to get involved in the kinds of arguments that can only rob us of our peace.

"God, yes, but not the Church," or "Oh, I believe in God, but I don't believe in organized religion," is something we hear often. I know from experience how futile it is to try to approach a closed heart: "Why do you not understand what I am saying? Because you cannot bear to hear my word" (Jn 8:43, NAB). But there are times when one is trapped and confronted with an unavoidable statement or question. We cannot call our clergy every time we encounter this situation. We should know how to defend God's word and the Church's teaching—we have an obligation to be prepared. Wherever we are, we know that God tells us through Paul that "by one Spirit we were all baptized into one body" (1 Cor 12:13, NKJ), and that "he put all things under his feet and gave him to be head over all things to the Church, which is his body, the fullness of him who fills all in all" (Eph 1:22–23, NKJ). Jesus founded the Church through Peter, giving her all authority (Mt 16:18) and promising that the Holy Spirit would be with the Church forever to keep her in the truth (Jn 16:13). Therefore, we must speak in the name of the Church's head, Jesus Christ, and try to lead Christians back to their respective Churches.

5. When "No, thank you, I'm all right" is only a partial "No"

When patients tell us that they "don't need anything," we in our hospital write "no" beside their names. Sometimes it is the mother of a new baby who tells me, "No, thanks, we are both healthy." Many of those relieved by the good outcome of an operation will not even think of joining you in a prayer of thanks; maybe they will say, "No, thanks, I'm leaving soon." Occasionally, when I ask if they need anything, they laughingly answer, "I hope not!" However, when their need for prayer is obvious I might say, "We can always use prayer," or "Would you mind if I pray for you?" An insecure, painful refusal of communion is not necessarily a refusal of prayer. If we want to do God's will and allow him to be in control, our prayer may be important in that person's life. One young woman, who had declined pastoral care, readily accepted my offer to pray. I held her hand and prayed, and she wiped the tears from her eyes, thanked me, and kissed my hand. When I pray with patients who join me in their hearts, I often lift up those others who seem to reject God when they reject me, knowing how much he loves them and how he is calling them.

Chapter 3 · Nonverbal Aspects of Pastoral Care

*The heart of a man changes his
countenance, either for good
or for evil (Sir 13:24–25, NAB)*

1. The environment and the people

If we act from the heart in our ministry, we become increasingly sensitive to all that communicates beyond words, both personally and environmentally. Nevertheless, it is good to outline the principal areas of nonverbal communication that are intimately related to pastoral care.

Beginning with the *room,* I suggest to student nurses as a project in my nonverbal communication courses that they observe and write about the eloquent sources of information they will find there—special cards, gifts, pictures of their loved ones (which, particularly for terminal patients, fill the long hours with their silent company), stuffed animals, religious or humorous get-well cards, flowers, no flowers, tabloids, jigsaw puzzles, crosswords books, romance novels, books on death and dying, mysteries, family magazines, textbooks, spiritual books, a Bible, a rosary, a radio or cassette player, the ubiquitous TV set, and the telephone to maintain some threads of communication with the world.

We can also learn a great deal from the *visitors:* those who seem deeply motivated; those whose hurried attitude may reflect the shallowness of their feelings for the patient; those who by not removing their coats tell the patient they do not want to stay long; those who pick up the reading material they find there, watch the television, or wander in and out of the room, never really maintaining true interaction; those who force the patient to discuss family finances that "must be taken care of"; those who lack compassion and communicate nonverbally their uneasiness and inability to cope with other people's suffering; and even members of the immediate family who do not seem to have a very close relationship with their suffering relative.

As for *personal appearance,* we may find those who are satisfied with, indifferent or resigned to, the hospital, and those who wear fine nightclothes that reflect their social background. Among the former, neglect of self might betray very low spirits or even depression. On the other hand, an excessive concern for appearance might be found in a manic-depressive woman in a manic phase.

In the *initial encounter,* I have yet to meet anyone who would not respond to eye contact. Even more, a handshake always has a positive effect on the encounter. Because of the uniqueness of each person, it can be futile to make participants in pastoral care workshops engage in role-playing. As in experimental psychology, pretending never yields what a real situation does, because we cannot feign what we would feel for an actual patient.

Another nonverbal aspect of visitation, suggested above, is the *presence or absence of people and things,* which communicate not only by their presence, but also by their absence. In some situations, words unuttered can be as important as those that are said, or things undone as vital as those that are done.

We tend to value words, gestures, objects—whatever we can apprehend with the senses, whatever "happens"—more than what is not said, is absent, or does not happen. Sometimes we find a patient whose room betrays loneliness, who has nothing tangible to show that he is remembered by relatives or friends, who has hardly any visitors or none at all. At the other extreme, we find a patient lavished with visits and all kinds of things: cards, flowers, fruit baskets, chocolates, magazines, balloons, stuffed animals. We should greet the lonely ones in the room, chatting with and ministering to them, and perhaps include them in our prayer, thus bringing them closer to their roommates before we attend to our patient.

2. How we say what we say

Speech is made up of three simultaneous or alternating channels of communication: "what we say," that is, words; "how we say it" with our voice; and "how we move it" with gestures, manners, and postures. We are generally conscious of our words, and may even select our vocabulary carefully as we speak to a patient, trying not to offend or instill fear or mistrust, but inspire hope, cheerfulness, and trust in God. If we interact with the love of Christ in our hearts, the Holy Spirit will help us just as he helped the prophets whom God wanted to speak to the people: "'Ah, Lord God!' I said, 'I know not how to speak; I am too young.'...Have no fear before them, because I am with you...'" (Jer 1:6, 8, NAB).

The way we say what we say is called "paralanguage." This supports, emphasizes, contradicts, or camouflages—consciously or unconsciously—what we are saying with words. It consists of four types of voice phenomena. First, a series of essential voice features such as: tempo, which should not be hurried as if we were thinking of leaving rather than staying, but calm; pitch, which should not deviate from what we normally use; intensity, which is indicative, for instance, when too loud, of a forced cheerfulness when there is nothing to be cheerful about. There are many possible types of voice we can adopt, each with a communicative function reflecting a specific attitude that the patient sometimes can interpret even better than ourselves (dull, lively, husky, tense, relaxed, soft). We should try to make it reflect love and inspire trust and a desire to communicate and share, always so therapeutic. Whispering, for instance, so appropriate for intimacy, is improper if a doctor and nurse were to whisper about a patient right outside the door. A patient's creaky voice might disclose pain or discomfort in addition to old age, while our own might betray boredom. A harsh voice, a gruff one, is far from being the voice of love, and tension could stimulate a patient's anxiety.

In addition, the sounds of certain physiological and psychological reactions including laughter, crying, shouting, sighing, coughing, even yawning, play unsuspected interactive functions. Laughter is not something we use just when something or someone is funny or because we are happy: "Even in laughter the heart may be sad" (Prv 14:13, NAB). There are forms of laughter that we use even when talking to a terminally ill person. There is the "support-seeking" type of laughter of many underprivileged and lonely people crying for affection, or the "compassionate laughter" displayed with seriously ill patients, which we could also verbalize with soothing words of understanding. At times, our support may simply consist in laughing about the unlaughable. At others, we hear nervous laughter that seeks relief from anxiety, triggered by a threatening concern the patient refuses to face and needs to deny; or "bittersweet laughter" that betrays mixed feelings and also shows on the face in an emotional blend. As for crying or weeping, a Christian professor of nursing tells us:

> Those in the helping professions, whether psychiatric, medical, or pastoral, have a unique opportunity to assist people in expressing "negative" emotions....[Crying is] a God-given

function which serves a useful purpose and should be thera-peutically supported by the Christian counselor....the human body can survive only limited amounts of stress. God in his providence has provided various tension releases, one of which is crying.[14]

The professor then quotes Stott:

Modern tearlessness is a misunderstanding of God's plan of salvation, a false assumption that his saving work is fin-ished...that there is no need for any more sickness, suffering, or sin, which are the causes of sorrow.[15]

She concludes that those who repress crying

foster emotional dishonesty and the wearing of masks among God's people...when they prevent the supportive "bearing of one another's burdens" (Gal 6:2).[16]

Besides many other instances of crying in the Bible (e.g., the sorrow of King Josiah at the people's unfaithfulness, in 2 Kings 22:19, or the repentant King David in Psalm 6:8), let us remember Jesus' sadness as Mary grieved over her brother Lazarus' death (Jn 11:35), or Peter's bitter tears after denying his master (Mt 26:75). Today we can witness the most unselfish and sublime cry-ing as a manifestation of conversion and repentance, a radical turning of a person's heart and mind to God through Jesus Christ by the power of the Holy Spirit: "a woman in the city who was a sinner...began to wash [Jesus'] feet with her tears" (Lk 7:37–38, NKJ). The Pentecostal pastor David Wilkerson gives us some excellent real-life examples of tears of repentance and conversion in his classic, *The Cross and the Switchblade.*[17]

Finally, within paralanguage we use a great number of word-like utterances, such as grunts of reluctant acceptance, "er" or "uh," that may reveal hesitation, audible inhalations and exhala-tions of anxiety, throat-clearings of embarrassment or tension, a sighed or higher-than-normal-pitched "mmm!" to fill an awkward silence. A heartfelt sigh with a commiserative tongue click may be all that we can say.

3. Gestures, manners, postures

Kinesics is the scientific term for "body language." Popular literature abounds in simplistic generalizations and shallow conclusions that totally ignore the deeper levels of personal interaction, as in, "If you lean back, or cross your arms, you are indicating lack of interest." We can lean forward and still show by the way our eyes wander occasionally or stare at a person that our mind is somewhere else. In other words, we interact in behavioral clusters; it is those combinations that convey messages and meanings, not any one behavior.

As for *gaze behavior,* it is good to remember that we should keep intermittent eye contact with the person with whom we interact, for feedback and to qualify our words and gestures. Through our interlocked glances, we establish better intimacy for confidentiality. We can better emphasize what we are trying to get across if we make eye contact. On occasion, we can even reach mutual understanding without words just by looking quietly at each other at an intimate distance sitting on the patient's bed. We should also know that we must never look someone in the eye when that person wants to disclose something very intimate, bring up a difficult or embarrassing subject, or recall painful memories. For that, we must grant them some "visual privacy." Also, we must never exchange knowing glances with others in front of patients, for they are more vulnerable than we imagine to whatever may communicate. They are aware

> of the importance of the *kind of eyes* they would see when awakening from their treatment. Eyes of love, care and concern differ from those which are impersonal or irritated and upset. One's eyes speak prayer.[18]

4. Communicating through silence, not fearing it

We communicate by the sound of our voice and the movements and positions of our bodies, but we cannot ignore the expressive potential of silence and stillness. Yet we do, especially silence. Why? We Westerners cannot bear interactive silences of more than a few seconds, since they trigger anxiety. Even in the Bible we can see how we dread God's "silence" when he does not seem to answer our prayers: "You see this, Lord; do not keep silent; do not withdraw from me" (Ps 35:22), "Do not keep silent, O God" (Ps 83:1, NAB). In Revelation 8:1 we feel the ominous silence when the seven angels are preparing to blow their trumpets before the series of woes: "When he opened the seventh seal, there was silence in heaven for about half an hour" (NKJ).

Silence is equated with solitude and loneliness. An elderly widow advised another who had just lost her husband, "You'll want to keep the television on!" Silence with visual contact causes even more anxiety because we feel that if we have eye contact we must say something, and if we are looked at, something, anything, must be said to us. That is why we try to camouflage it and, in order to fill what we see as a void, say something trivial or clear our throat. Are we not afraid of silence even when we come before God in prayer and cannot even stop the words being uttered in our minds? As Blessed Faustina wrote in her *Diary:*

> Silence is so powerful a language that it reaches the throne of the living God. Silence is his language, though secret, yet living and powerful (#888). In silence I tell you everything, Lord, because the language of love is without words (#1489).

Most of those pauses that occur in conversation are far from being just voids. Even if nothing is said verbally, we may be sending all kinds of bodily messages through a subtle facial expression, a commiserative shake of the head, glistening eyes, or a blush. We must realize that a meaningful silence is not a void or gap in our visit, but something that is an important part of any interaction, an eloquent, wordless statement of our concern and love for the patient when true rapport has been achieved and no verbalization is needed.

Swiss psychiatrist Paul Tournier gives a moving example of the therapeutic use of silence and of time. In one of his inspiring books he tells of a doctor who was called to see a critically ill patient. She realized that the patient did not want a flood of words from her—he wanted real, deep, burning companionship. She spent a whole hour of complete silence with him, and now that hour is for her one of the most beautiful of her life.[19]

The Book of Ecclesiastes assures us that there is "a time to be silent, and a time to speak" (Eccl 3:7, NAB), and this is exactly what will happen if we act with the discernment that the Spirit will give us when we truly desire and allow ourselves to be led by him.

5. Interpersonal distance and touch

One important nonverbal aspect of pastoral care is what in social interaction is called *proxemics*, the study of interpersonal spacing and touch. In pastoral care, it means the distance we keep from our patients while visiting and how we establish physical contact with them. I usually sit on the side of the bed after I discern the kind of person I am facing. Sometimes I ask permission, other times I do not. With some patients I never sit on the bed, regardless of their sex, age, or condition. With the right person at the right time, the mere fact that I sit there on my own initiative can develop an instant bond of sharing created by acting naturally with a person who welcomes the closeness of a compassionate heart.

Throughout the Bible, touch has a close association with compassion and the healing miracles. Elijah, Elisha, and Paul stretched themselves out upon the dead (1 Kgs 17:21; 2 Kgs 4:35; Acts 20:10). In various ways Jesus touched people to heal them and in at least one case "everyone in the crowd sought to touch him because power came forth from him and healed them all" (Lk 6:19, NAB).

I always shake hands with patients, many times I lay my hand on theirs, and I almost always hold their hand while praying because, as Francis MacNutt says, I want to "pray *with* people instead of just *for* them."[20] Many times I will feel their hand squeezing mine, for they can sense my love for them. Once I happened not to do this while praying with Norbert, a retired Air Force officer, but when I finished he reached for my closed hand and gave it a warm squeeze. I do it least frequently in the psychiatric unit, lest it should lead to misinterpretation or elicit unwanted feelings, and in Maternity, unless I can see a clear need or a very open personality. I have also been able to sense the basic need for that physical "with-ness" in how they accept my wordless suggestion to hold hands to pray: in how easily they put their other hand over mine; in how a mature man past the prejudices of youth takes the initiative on my second visit; or in how, when I hold a young man's hand or forearm to pray, he and his girlfriend clasp each other's hand, thankful for the visit.

On the other hand, let us not forget that there are marked differences in proxemic behavior and touch among cultures. Some are used to much physical contact (Lebanese, Hispanics, Italians, Greeks, French, Indians, Russians, Arabs); others, to much less (Northern Europeans, English); and still others to practically none after early childhood (Japan, Malaysia). The languages of Ghana do not even have a word for "kissing." However, at a Roman Catholic charismatic prayer group of about a hundred people in Tokyo, brothers and sisters of both sexes and all ages embraced as lovingly as I have seen Christians of many cultures do. I had the same experience among the physicians attending the conference of Christian Medical Foundation.

6. The patient's time and our time

Another nonverbal aspect of pastoral care is the duration of our visits and of what we do with our time there: feeding someone (not necessarily our patient) rather than calling a nurse when we see that they cannot do it easily themselves, arranging pillows, taking a wheelchair-bound patient somewhere, or guiding someone to a quiet room for communion and prayer. A student in one of my nonverbal communication courses studied the *chronemics*—that is, the conceptualization, perception, and structure of time in social interaction—of a senior-citizen home. She commented on the time environment of the patients and the difference between the two types of time: the actual clock time of residents and of the staff and visitors who came in contact with them, and the "psychological time," or how time is perceived: as very short when we are having a good time or unbearably long if we are waiting.

Since this ministry is to Jesus himself, as he assures us, I soon realized that I had to give of myself and never hurry. It is better not to accept this responsibility than to carry it out in a rush. Each individual deserves the time he or she needs, no more and no less. We should try not to look as if we have the next patient in mind, but should measure time by our heart, not our watch.

Being generous with our time may mean returning to a room more than once if necessary. I first found Pat, a cancer patient, talking on the telephone, then twice napping, but when I returned the fourth time, we visited and I prayed with her. I found that she wanted communion that day, and she was very grateful for my visit. We feel drawn to visit some patients on days when we are not scheduled to be in the hospital. This can be more than a "feeling"; it can be of the Spirit. Perhaps that day other visitors were unable for some reason to bring communion to a patient who expected it or who truly needed prayer, or relatives were looking for us or for a priest. God gives us the unexpected and we should always be thankful for it.

Chapter 4 ·
Prayer and Scripture
in Pastoral Care

My word...shall not return to me void, but shall do my will,
achieving the end for which I sent it (Is 55:11, NAB)

1. Our personal prayer time

Our own prayer life will be reflected in our ministry to the patients: the more filled we are of the Spirit, the more we will be able to give ourselves to others. Many find that their best prayer time is in the morning. It equips us for the day ahead, and the Bible tells us, "My voice you shall hear in the morning, O Lord; In the morning I will direct it to you" (Ps 5:3/4, NKJ),[21] "In the morning my prayer comes before you" (Ps 88:13, NAB), "One must rise before the sun to give thee thanks, and must pray to thee at the dawning of the light" (Wis 16:28, RSV), "Morning by morning he wakens my ear" (Is 50:4, NKJ), and Jesus himself "in the morning...before daylight...he prayed" (Mk 1:35, NKJ).

One of the most difficult things with which we cope is going from the workplace–where we may be nagged by people and situations that threaten our peace—to the hospital where people face sickness, death, and ultimately God eternal. It is different to go to the hospital directly from home, where we may have just prayed and read scripture. That is why it is always necessary to prepare ourselves through prayer, keeping in mind that we are going to join those patients, and must therefore protect ourselves, our heart and our minds, from whatever might undermine the efficacy of our ministry.

2. When we don't feel up to visiting

It can happen that we arrive at the hospital burdened by something we should not have brought with us that makes us feel unworthy to minister to our brothers and sisters in Jesus' name. It is a terrible feeling.

One night I was feeling miserable. I even skipped my time for prayer with my wife because I did not make the effort, as I have other times, to sit and join her in prayer. Nothing good could come from that. The following morning, as I opened the tabernacle in our hospital chapel, I knelt and prayed:

> Lord Jesus, forgive me for coming like this. I know I am even more unworthy than at other times to serve my brothers and sisters on these floors. But, Lord, I am afraid I am the only thing you've got this morning, nothing better. So, Lord, I beg you not to let those people suffer the consequences of my sin. Forgive me and cleanse me, Lord. Let me go with your blessing, Lord. I love you, Lord, in my weakness and nothingness. Thank you, Lord.

I went up to my first floor. My first patient was in Palliative Care, a woman with great faith and trust in God. I explained how I was feeling and she lifted me up just by talking about herself. Later, in Pediatrics, I met a smiling five-year-old girl, for whom we were praying at home. I felt Jesus' love for her, and the cloud lifted from my heart and mind. God is so faithful, "so great is his faithfulness" (Lam 3:23, NAB).

Another day I had some very special visits, particularly one with a whole family whose father's name should have been on my list, but was not. First, I was led to talk to one of the sons in the corridor and I learned that his father was dying and was a Catholic. The family encouraged me to go in before I offered to. The room was full of silent relatives; only the father's labored breath was heard. I prayed for him, touching my pyx (the small box with the consecrated wafers) to his chest. I prayed that they would offer his suffering and their own suffering to Jesus, who died for that man and for each one of us. I prayed that God would give them peace. We all prayed the Our Father and the Hail Mary, and five or six of the relatives received communion.

Now I know that if I ever arrive at the hospital burdened by something that obviously does not come from God, it will begin to lift like morning fog if I kneel before the Holy Sacrament. Minutes later Jesus will meet me wherever I go. Once I asked Mother Teresa, as we watched her sisters coming out of the mother house's chapel in Calcutta, how they have the strength to do what they do day in and day out. She answered, looking at the tabernacle, "Only receiving Jesus in communion can give them the strength every morning."

3. Praying before visitation

The next step is preparation before visitation. Whether we are part of a small team or minister individually, we should pray from the heart in this vein:

> Father, we come before you with praise and thanks for allowing us to minister to our brothers and sisters in the name of your Son Jesus, and to ask you to bless each of our visits. Free us from all the distractions we bring from outside and fill us with your Spirit so that we may minister to them

according to your will. We lift them up to you, Lord Jesus, knowing how much you love them. Prepare their hearts and minds and be with us in those rooms. We pray especially for the new patients, that they may not reject you, Lord, and for those who do. Holy Spirit, be with us, pray with us. And, Mother Mary, we ask for your intercession, knowing that you want only to bring them closer to your Son. In Jesus' name. Amen.

We must trust in God's mercy, asking him to open the hearts of those patients, knowing that, whatever happens later, he hears our prayer before visitation. We remember how God "opened [Lydia's] heart to pay attention to what Paul was saying" (Acts 16:14, NAB).

4. Praying with the patient: Verbal and nonverbal aspects

There are two intimately related components in our prayer with the patients, nonverbal and verbal. Without words, we communicate an attitude by either sitting on their bed or standing while we pray. Each person is different. No explanation is necessary just to hold a hand or clasp a shoulder. Sometimes it is good to justify touching a bad leg, arm, or back simply by a reference to Jesus' words, "They will lay hands on the sick" (Mk 16:18, NAB). That example from Jesus himself may be a discovery for many as we make them aware of the legitimacy of such a basic biblical and Christian way of praying with someone. Again, not once have I sensed the least discomfort in a patient because of touching: on the contrary, sometimes their own hand squeezing, seeking, or lingering on mine expresses their feelings, with or without words.

As for oral prayer, the best is undoubtedly spontaneous, just as we talk to the Father and to Jesus when we pray in private, presenting the needs of the patient simply and according to their specific needs. No two will be alike. Even among those suffering from the same illness, one takes it well and with faith; another feels anxious, depressed, or despondent; another is gripped by fear; another is the victim of past hurts; another is lonely; still another grieves over a loved one. There will be times when we may be at a loss, not knowing what is ailing a patient besides illness. But if we pray: "Lord, I lift up to you my brother's/sister's needs," acknowledging his love and mercy, we know that "He who searches the hearts knows what the mind of the Spirit is, because he makes intercession for the saints according to the will of God" (Rom 8:27, NKJ). At other times, we might be asked to pray for something other than what concerns the illness. Once, after we prayed for a woman, her husband asked me to please pray for a serious financial situation in which he was being treated very unjustly.

Although I always pray spontaneously and differently with each person, I like to begin by saying, "Thank you, Lord for bringing me to my sister/brother_____," very often following it with something such as this:

> We thank you, Jesus, for your presence because we know that you always fulfill your promises, and you said, "When two or more are gathered together in my name, I am in their midst." So, Lord, _____ and I thank you for that presence.

If for some reason I sense I should be brief and perhaps only give communion, I will begin, "Let us come for a moment into the presence of the Lord. My brother/sister_____ and I thank you, Lord...." Even when we are not accustomed to spontaneous prayer we can be sure that if we engage in this ministry out of love for the Lord and for the patients, we will easily learn to verbalize what we are saying in our heart in a way that will naturally vary with each person. The Holy Spirit will give us words, helping us grow in this important form of prayer.

Often we might go to see a patient only to find that he or she is busy with the doctor or nurse, and we may or may not be able to return. Sometimes we sense that he or she is very much in need of prayer. The fact that we cannot approach the patient is no excuse to walk away without having prayed with them. The first time I found someone in strict isolation in Intensive Care, I stood at the glass door, facing him, and lifted him up to God. On other occasions it has happened that, because of the seriousness of her condition, I would not approach the patient to say anything.

Once I visited a middle-aged woman who had many stitches in her neck and was terribly nauseated. I only said that I was from pastoral care and would return later. I stood outside the door and asked God to ease her and allow her to rest. A few minutes later I looked in on her and she was peacefully asleep. We see in both instances that if the patient obviously needs prayer nothing can stop us from lifting that person up to God and, as always, leave the results to him.

5. Our personal reading of the Bible

If one prerequisite for personalized, spontaneous prayer with patients is our own personal prayer, we should realize that both kinds of prayer, and therefore our ministry to the sick, will be much deeper and richer if we complement them with prayerful daily reading of the Bible, the word of God, where he speaks to each of us personally. We cannot just hear it when it is read in church, because "to ignore the scriptures is to ignore Christ."[22]

Andrew Murray, the great South African devotional writer and pastor in the Reformed Church, who spoke and wrote much about prayer and "the sin of prayerlessness," emphasized that our prayerful study of the Bible is indispensable for powerful prayer.[23] Our prayer with those who suffer needs to be powerful not in voice, but in depth, and in intimate contact with Jesus and with the Father. Thus we need to know the mind of the God of the Old Testament, a loving Father who constantly calls us, his people, in order to sanctify us and prepare us for salvation, who announced the coming of Jesus hundreds of years before it happened, and gave us the truth for all times to answer any question about him, ourselves, and others. Jesus tells us that "Man shall not live by bread alone, but by every word that proceeds from the mouth of God" (Mt 4:4, NKJ; Dt 8:3); thus, reading the Bible is a necessity, not an option.

If a Christian should read the Bible regularly, how much more should those dedicated to serving their brothers and sisters in pastoral care, in order to draw from the endless wellspring of God's word, where we find God (Father, Son, and Holy Spirit) as our protector (Ps 18:2/3), our "wonderful counselor" (Is 9:6, RSV), our teacher (Mt 23:10, NKJ), our comforter (2 Cor 1:3), and our guide (Acts 13:4). There are many occasions in our ministry when we need to cling to "the sword of the Spirit, which is the word of God" (Eph 6:17, NAB), knowing exactly what we want to say. It is only through our own daily reading of scripture that we will have enough wisdom to confront situations with the discernment to know what is good and what is wrong and what goes against God's commandments. How can we fulfill our obligation to be God's witnesses if we cannot convey what the Bible says about something, even generally, since "faith comes by hearing, and hearing by the word of God" (Rom 10:17, NKJ)?

6. Working from and with scripture

Having reflected on the intimate relationship between prayer and personal reading of the Bible, it follows that God's word is an indispensable tool in pastoral care.

My first day at the hospital I forgot my Bible. I missed it. I knew that most of the time I would not actually read it but quote or paraphrase it. However, if I discreetly carry my Bible with me, I know that I can open it, read from it, and show how the Lord wants to speak to, for instance, a new mother and baby with Psalm 139:13–16, always a happy discovery for parents in Maternity.

I would find my ministry difficult if I were unfamiliar with the word of God and did not make it a point to read it daily. How many times, after reading it prayerfully in the morning, have I had the opportunity to share it with someone? It is a great blessing in pastoral ministry because we often read just what we will need later for specific patients. It is also a way of keeping them in touch with the Church, particularly on a Sunday.

One Sunday, a patient told me he did not want communion because he had been away from the Church for many years. The gospel reading of the day was Matthew 20:1-16, about the workers in the vineyard. At other times, to assure a despondent or cynical patient of God's love for someone "like him," I may resort to Luke 15:1-7, the parable of the lost sheep, or what follows in the rest of Luke 15, the parable of the prodigal son. We can be sure that if the scriptures are our daily bread, God will tell us, as he did Ezekiel, when he made him eat the scroll, "Go now to the house of Israel, and speak my words to them" (Ez 2:4, NAB). We will undoubtedly be better equipped to carry out our ministry, since

> all scripture is inspired by God and profitable for teaching, for reproof, for correction, and for training in righteousness, that the man of God may be complete, fully equipped for every good work (2 Tm 3:16-17).

And equipped we must be at all times with "the helmet of salvation, and the sword of the Spirit, which is the word of God" (Eph 6:17, NKJ), knowing that

> the word of God is living and active…, piercing to the division of soul and spirit…, discerning the thoughts and intentions of the heart (Heb 4:12).

The former psychiatric nurse Barbara Shlemon, today well known in the healing ministry and as a Catholic speaker, encourages "volunteer visitors to the sick" by reporting to "have heard countless testimonies from people whose illness began to disappear as they invoked the power of a scripture passage."[24]

I am not suggesting an indiscriminate approach with the Bible, but that we be fully conscious of its important function in pastoral care, not only for pastoral care workers or for the clergy, but for medical practitioners themselves, doctors and nurses, with whom we form a team attending to the whole person. That is why nurses Sharon Fish and Judith Allen Shelly emphasize that "one of the nurse's personal resources is knowledge of the scripture...to be able to comfort and use scripture therapeutically," attested by medical bodies such as Christian Medical Foundation and the Association of Christian Therapists. I must hasten to add that we cannot read scripture indiscriminately to those who suffer.

> Applying Bible passages too quickly can create unnecessary barriers to communication...increase further expression of needs...communicate an impersonal God who has a pat answer to every question but refuses to concern himself with the real feelings and frustrations of suffering human beings who need compassionate understanding. For a patient who has little knowledge of the Bible and may be questioning God's existence and involvement in his life, pat answers from scripture can serve to alienate him further from God.[25]

There is nothing we cannot find in scripture. God even seems to warn us against quoting it at the wrong time in Job's sarcastic reaction to his friends' attempt to teach him in the middle of his suffering without empathizing with him: "No doubt you are the intelligent folk, and with your wisdom shall die!" (Jb 12:2, NAB). So we must be careful when, how, and to whom we convey God's words, since, used at the wrong time, they may do more harm than good and we may hear someone echo Job: "I have heard this sort of things many times. Wearisome comforters are you all!" (Jb 16:2, NAB). However, having warned their colleagues against using the Bible indiscriminately. Fish and Shelly encourage them to resort to what they call "identification passages," relating different passages in which the patients could identify with the situations and needs expressed in them.

The advice offered by these authors suggests, therefore, that pastoral caregivers should discern when one has to allow God to speak directly to their patients, for, when the word is used according to his will, God says: "It shall not return to me void, but shall do my will, achieving the end for which I sent it" (Is 55:11). How many times have I seen this! When I was faced with an extremely anxious young man, I invited him to sit with me as I tried to soothe him, I read Romans 8:28, Philippians 4:6–7, and Psalm 139:13–16 and his anxiety subsided.

I must add that frequently and significantly having my Bible in the hospital is something that fosters good rapport and understanding between non-Catholics and me and between them and my Catholic patients.

7. Fasting as a biblical complement to prayer

Does the very mention of fasting sound like an exaggeration in the context of pastoral care visitation? Not if we continue to intercede for our sick brothers and sisters in our own prayer time.

> I, when they were ill...afflicted myself with fasting, sobbed my prayers upon my bosom (Ps 35:13).

We might habitually keep a day of fasting during the week as many Christians do, in which case we can offer it for patients; or we may decide to make a little extra effort in a particular case. We know that fasting is God's prescribed complement to prayer, as the book of Tobit tells us:

> Prayer is good when accompanied by fasting, almsgiving, and righteousness (Tb 12:8).

Throughout the Old Testament we find numerous teachings on the objectives and effects of fasting, either privately or collectively: in bereavement (2 Sm 1:12), for protection (Ezr 8:21; Est 4:16; 2 Chr 20:2-3), in repentance (1 Kgs 21:22, 27; Jl 2:12; Jon 3:5), for petition (2 Sm 12:15-16, though ineffectual in God's will for David), and for intercession (Ps 35:13; Dn 9:3). In the New Testament, Jesus, who assures us, "Do not think that I have come to abolish the law or the prophets. I have come not to abolish but to fulfill" (Mt 5:17, NAB), himself fasts to gain strength in the Spirit (Mt 4:2), tells us how to fast (Mt 6:16-18), admonishes us for not doing it (Mt 17:21; Mk 9:29), and clarifies for us that now, after he has redeemed us on the cross, is the time to fast (Mt 9:15).

Later we see how his apostles, following the Old Testament tradition and their master's example, reinforced their prayer with fasting (Acts 13:2-3, 14:23, 15:23), and Saint Paul mentions it as a meritorious act "as ministers of God" (2 Cor 6:4, NAB). In the *Didache,* or *Teaching of the Apostles,*[26] the earliest known Christian writing apart from the New Testament, fasting is recommended on Wednesdays and Fridays. For John Wesley, the great eighteenth-century founder of the Methodist Church, it was a condition for the ordination of ministers, and the English king of his time called for a day of prayer and fasting (as does King Jehoshaphat in 2 Chronicles 20:2-3) to ward off a French invasion. Pope Paul VI encouraged us to fast in his encyclical on penance.

Today, fasting is done according to each individual's capacity and has renewed prominence in the ordinary spiritual life of many Christians, who have discovered its fruits.[27] Pastoral care workers can also enrich their own spiritual life and the effectiveness of their ministry and intercession by offering this personal sacrifice to the Lord.

8. Pastoral care and nonprofessional counseling

The guidelines I received as a Catholic lay pastoral care volunteer state that we are "to assist the priests of the area in meeting the physical, psychological, social and spiritual needs of patients and their families during the period of illness or injury...referring patients to professional people (like priests...) when it would appear that counseling is necessary."

Most of us are not professional counselors and should not be too ready to assume that responsibility, nor to usurp the role of the clergy. But sometimes pastoral visitation requires a bit of what can only be called counseling.

For instance, I may find some grieving relatives in Intensive Care. While I may have prayed with the patient, what they need at that moment is what could be called spiritual counseling, for instance, about God's unconditional and unquestionable love for the patient, his allowing events to take place, Jesus' suffering on the cross for that person, and the family's need to heed the words in Philippians 4:7 and seek that peace of God "that surpasses all understanding [and] will guard your hearts and minds in Christ Jesus" (NAB). Naturally, one cannot approach all grieving relatives the same way, but with experience, one can see what form of prayer they will appreciate. If we allow the Spirit to lead us, we can be sure that he will inspire in us the right prayer for the right people at the right time.

We should not take the initiative to counsel, unless we sense great anxiety that we know might be relieved by talking, which I have experienced many times. There are also times when we should refer the patient to our clergy. Leading them to the clergy often requires a bit of preliminary counseling if they bring up a particular issue or start sharing their problems. At that point there are two alternatives: avoid expressing an opinion or giving advice, and just listen, sympathize, and be discreet, detached, and rather useless, instead of accepting our poverty and acting through it; or we can help our brothers and sisters by using the discernment we have gained through knowledge of scripture and, for a Roman Catholic, of the *Catechism,* much of which applies to all Christians.

There are times when I tell the patients they should speak to a priest, particularly when I see, for instance, that sacramental confession is the answer, or that they have been away from the Church for a long time. Often, because they are not ready, they do not want to talk to a priest—yet we may be able to lead them to one. If I feel in my heart that I am aiding the priest in this ministry, I just say what I must and leave the results to the Lord. When we know that what we say is not founded on the world's way of seeing things but on God's way and his word, we cannot go wrong.

Once, a young woman told me she had not attended church for years and that she did not feel like asking for communion. I could not help seeing in her the stray sheep approaching the sheepfold. I spoke to her of God's great love for her, of her commitment as a Catholic who had once received the sacraments, and of how much better she would feel if she decided to come back, contact a priest, and live as a Christian in her Church. The following morning, as her husband was about to take her home, they both spoke to me in very friendly terms and he said she had spoken to him about me. Would it have been better if I had refrained from "counseling" her in the absence of a more "professional" person?

On another occasion, only after speaking quite a few times with a young man and giving him several things to read, could I lead him to see a priest for confession, to start attending mass and receiving communion. We should again remember that God tells us in Isaiah 55:11: "[My word] shall not return to me empty, but it shall accomplish that which I purpose, and prosper in the thing for which I sent it" (RSV). We can try to plant the seed and God will make it grow if it is his will.

There are plenty of Bible-based materials from which we can benefit immensely for this type of circumstantial "counseling." Roman Catholics have the new *Catechism,* a doctrinal treasury each Catholic pastoral care worker should be familiar with, just as they should be familiar with the pope's encyclicals, which he writes for all of us. Often patients ask questions on morals, for which the *Catechism* and the 1993 encyclical *Veritatis Splendor (The Splendor of Truth)* contain the answers, and we, as Catholics ministering to them, have an obligation to answer them. Sometimes this counseling may require some follow-up, allowing them time to ponder our conversation or to read something we lend them and give us some feedback. We may do that outside our regular visiting time.

Once I encountered a patient who had already received bad "counseling." She told me she did not attend church on Sunday anymore because her strict Catholic friends had told her she could not attend mass because she was divorced. I was indignant and pained, seeing her state of bitterness and guilt. I assured her that she could certainly attend mass and receive the sacraments, if she was not married again without an annulment, and that she could and should avail herself of the sacrament of reconciliation, and I encouraged her to see a priest.

We cannot be "dummies" when patients share with us things they carry deep in their hearts that hurt them more than they realize. How can we prove that we are compassionate listeners if we do not externalize that compassion? Naturally, we must be prepared and grounded in the word of God. This knowledge is acquired by regular daily reading and meditating on scripture, as Christians are supposed to do, and by reading Bible-based literature.

Many issues, impossible to outline here, come up during our visits when we least expect them. Let us mention just one whose spiritual dimension is ignored by most people: smoking. I have seen patients with lung cancer who cannot free themselves from that bondage, and one of my first students died from heavy smoking. I remember a Christian Medical Foundation surgeon showing his colleagues lung tissue from an ordinary female smoker and saying with a lump in his throat, "If only they believed us!" To encourage smokers to give it up, I tell them how my own wife, who smoked for twenty years and was unable to quit despite her strong will power, succeeded when she faced God with a cigarette in her hand and said, "Lord, if you want me to stop, you do it. I cannot!" She put it down and never smoked again. As for the moral gravity of smoking, I refer to Paul's words, "Do you not know that your body is a temple of the Holy Spirit within you, whom you have from God, and that you are not your own?" (1 Cor 6:19, NAB). The *Catechism* says, "Life and physical health are precious gifts entrusted to us by God. We must take reasonable care of them, taking into account the needs of others and the common good" (#2288), and must "avoid every kind of excess: the abuse of food, alcohol, tobacco, or medicine" (#2290). If we desire to do God's will and help others do it as well, we will be able to be witnesses of his promise:

> The Lord God has given me a well-trained tongue, that I might know how to speak to the weary a word that will rouse them (Is 50:4, NAB).

Chapter 5 ·
The Sacramental Ministry
in Pastoral Care

"Take, eat; this is my body
which is broken for you; do this in
remembrance of me" (1 Cor 11:24, NKJ)

1. Communion: Our awe as ministers of the Eucharist and the re-education of the faithful

The early Church regarded the Eucharist as the ordinary sacrament of healing, since our Lord Jesus Christ becomes one with us so that we can say, "Christ lives in me" (Gal 2:20, NAB). Through the Eucharist, he wills to be one with us both physically and spiritually. On the value of communion as a source of strength for those who suffer, we have the private revelations to Blessed Faustina Kowalska:

> Understand that the strength by which you bear sufferings comes from frequent communions. So approach this fountain of mercy often, to draw with the vessel of trust whatever you need.[28]

How much better could we profit from this wonderful mystery if we always received Christ's body as we should, even expecting healing of our infirmities of body, mind, and heart. The *Catechism*, referring to Jesus' mandate, "Heal the sick" (Mt 10:8, NKJ), assures us:

> The life-giving presence of Christ, the physician of souls and bodies...in an altogether special way through the Eucharist, the bread that gives eternal life and that Saint Paul suggests is connected with bodily health (#1509).

That is why the famous fifteenth-century German writer Thomas à Kempis tells us:

> So great sometimes is this grace that from the abundance of the devotion that is bestowed not only the mind, but the frail body also feels a great increase of strength.[29]

In her *Way of Perfection*, one of the mystical works of the sixteenth-century Doctor of the Church, Teresa of Ávila relates how many times she would be freed of physical pain right after receiving "the most sacred bread" (XXXIV.6), for, as she writes:

> If when he lived in this world, the sick were healed by just touching his garments, what doubt is there but that he will work miracles, being so deeply within me, if we have faith, and that he will grant us whatever we ask, since he is in our home? (XXXIV.8)...Do not miss such a good opportunity of negotiating with him as after having received communion (XXXIV.10).[30]

Today, the Spirit-filled Irish nun Sr. Briege McKenna, writing on the Eucharist, relates some astonishing miracles she has seen during mass.[31] Often when I give communion I emphasize the words, "...and I shall be healed." What a great instrument of love and compassion in pastoral care is this, along with the word of God! The first day I carried my pyx I was overwhelmed by the great privilege of carrying Jesus' body, as his priests do. I thought of the words of the thirteenth-century saint, Francis of Assisi, in his *Admonitions,* on the real presence of Jesus in the Blessed Sacrament:

> Every day he humbles himself...in this sacred bread just as he once appeared to his apostles in real flesh. With their own eyes they saw only his flesh, but they believed that he was God because they contemplated him with the eyes of the spirit. We, too,...see only bread and wine, but we must see further and firmly believe that this is his most holy body and blood, living and true. In this way our Lord remains continually with his followers, as he promised, Behold, I am with you all days, even until the consummation of the world. (Mt 28:20)[32]

In her *Life,* St. Teresa, who had frequent visions of Jesus, tells us how she felt about receiving him in communion:

> When I approached communion and remembered that greatest majesty that I had seen, and thought of how it was the same one who was in the Most Blessed Sacrament, and many times the Lord wants me to see him in the host too, my hair stood on end and felt as if I were being overpowered. O my Lord! (XXXVIII.19)[33]

A century later, St. Margaret Mary Alacoque wrote of how she yearned to become a religious in order to be able to receive communion more often, and what she felt:

> On the eves of communion I found myself rapt in so profound a silence, on account of the greatness of the action I was about to perform, that I could not speak without great effort; and afterwards I would have wished neither to eat nor drink, to see nor speak, owing to the greatness of the consolation and peace which I then felt.[34]

By the relationship we establish with our patients as we take communion to them, we will be able to measure our relationship with God, for in this unique task, which we perform in service to him, we respond to the commandment, "You shall love your neighbor as yourself" (Lv 19:18, NAB), confirmed by Jesus (Mt 5:43).

We should not offer the Lord's body indiscriminately. Let us first ascertain that the patients are practicing Catholics who feel ready to receive communion. I may mention that a priest will come to them if they wish, by whom someone could return to the sacraments, maybe even to the Church. Above all, let us not sell the Lord's body cheaply. We learn by experience to detect the casualness with which some receive communion. As a rule, if we find a person watching a distracting or offensive television show or in the middle of a meal, we should bring the Eucharist some other time, lest we give the body of Christ under inappropriate conditions.

Once I was able to talk to a man about that kind of difficult situation, but he understood without taking offense and did not seem to mind at all when I said I should not give him communion. He accepted my laying hands on him and praying, after which I spoke to a priest.

The unthinking familiarity with which we may come to the Eucharist, together with our own spiritual immaturity, can turn it into a lukewarm Sunday or daily routine, "not being drawn," as Kempis says, "with greater affection to the receiving of Christ"; or, even worse, when "from daily use [our heart] falls into disregard of it."[35] We can advise patients to await communion at a certain time and avoid too much distraction when they are expecting us.

2. Praying before communion

As Eucharistic ministers, we have the responsibility to help our patients to see that "we must *prepare ourselves* for so great and so holy a moment" (*CCC,* #1385). The fact that there is so much casualness toward communion in Church does not mean that we must neglect to help our patients realize that "The principal fruit of receiving the Eucharist in holy communion is an intimate union or 'communication' with Christ Jesus." (*CCC,* #1391). No wonder Sr. Faustina wrote, "The most solemn moment of my life is the moment when I receive holy communion." In fact, Jesus revealed to her:

> But I want to tell you that eternal life must begin already here on earth through holy communion. Each holy communion makes you more capable of communing with God through eternity.[36]

In addition, St. Teresa tells us how the Lord blessed her so abundantly with visions after communion. Often, with certain patients, I include in my prayer before communion something like this:

> Lord Jesus, we thank you for the great gift you give us through our Catholic Church of being able to receive your body, the same body that died on the cross for each one of us. We ask you, Holy Spirit, to make us realize that we are receiving Jesus our Lord into our body. Make us more and more aware of this wonderful mystery that we may receive your body, Jesus, with the awe and the reverence and the gratitude you deserve. We thank you, Father, that you gave us your Son Jesus out of your great love for each one of us. We thank you, Jesus, that you allow us to receive you.

I also like to precede the words "This is the Lamb of God" with "This is Jesus," or "This is the body and blood of Jesus." Once I saw a priest in New Brunswick celebrating mass with true fervor and preaching "as one having authority" (Mt 7:29, NAB), who said those latter words, and later told me with glowing face, "I am in love with the Eucharist!" Isn't it our mission to propagate this love of Jesus and the wonderful mystery of communion?

3. Praying after communion

St. Teresa of Avila advises that after receiving communion one should "endeavor to close the eyes of the body and open those of the soul, and look into your heart."[37] And Thomas à Kempis says:

> You ought not only to prepare yourself by devotion before communion, but carefully also to keep yourself therein after receiving the sacrament....Beware of much talk, remain in secret and enjoy your God; for you have him whom all the world cannot take from you.[38]

To promote the appropriate reverence at a time when patients find themselves receiving communion in an environment which is not the familiar one of the church, I find it very helpful to remain in silence and with my eyes closed for a minute or two in order to avoid opening any communication channels. I may audibly praise and thank Jesus for the reception of his body, in which some patients join me quite readily. Sometimes, at this very special moment, I repeat any important point we may have mentioned in our prayer, such as the impending operation, the pain they are experiencing, or their recovery. Some pastoral caregivers, after a brief moment, may like to read a prayer or an appropriate scripture passage. Often, as I prepare to give communion, I advise them that I will go after they receive it and leave them with the Lord. This always suggests, I find, that moment of recollection during which they should avoid going back to their reading or television too soon, or to conversation with another patient or with a visitor, who may have received communion as well.

4. The anointing of the sick: Sacrament and sacramental

I would like to mention the anointing of the sick because many people still hold to the pre-Vatican II concept of the "extreme unction," or "last rites," ominous terms that evoke impending death and make the priest the messenger of death. However, it was restored as the true sacrament of healing by Vatican II. It is to be given "not [only] at the moment of death, but as soon as there is some danger of death from sickness or old age,"[39] for the person's recovery, as instituted by Jesus when he first sent his apostles. He "gave them power over unclean spirits....And [they] anointed with oil many who were sick, and healed them" (Mk 6:7, 13, NKJ). Since the very beginning of the Church, it was part of the healing ministry. The apostle James urged the sick to seek the presbyters of the Church: "Let them pray over him, anointing him with oil in the name of the Lord; and the prayer of faith will save the sick man" (Jas 5:14–15, NKJ).

Barbara Shlemon resigned as a psychiatric nurse in the mid-1960s. She went into a ministry of intercession precisely after seeing a dying cancer patient, for whose healing she had prayed, literally recover overnight after receiving the sacrament of the sick.[40] When the bishop consecrates the oil used in this sacrament, he says, "Lord God, loving Father, you bring healing to the sick....send the Holy Spirit...upon this oil...that they may be free from pain and illness, and made well again in body, mind, and soul," and so God always honors this sacrament according to his will, whether the results are physical or spiritual.

At the same time, there is the nonsacramental anointing of a sick person with blessed oil. Any of us can use it at home or elsewhere, as many of us have been encouraged to do after being anointed at a conference or healing mass and given a little vial of oil. Many pastoral care workers use this sacramental and anoint patients, after explaining, if necessary, the difference between the sacrament and the sacramental.

5. The sacrament of reconciliation and nonsacramental confession

The Roman Catholic and Orthodox Churches preserve penance as a sacrament. The Anglican Communion allows private nonsacramental confession to a priest. Other churches believe in the person's act of repentance and reconciliation with God, either in their own private prayer or also by sharing with a brother or sister: "Confess your sins to one another and pray for one another" (Jas 5:16, NAB), "If we acknowledge our sins, he is faithful and just and will forgive our sins" (1 Jn 1:9, NAB).

Catholic pastoral care visitors sometimes encounter people who, in the course of the conversation, begin to share their concerns, pains, and what they regard as sins. We should not try to avoid this spontaneous sharing, knowing how therapeutic it can be. We can try to help them with the words that any Christian Church would have for them. This I consider a basic Christian duty that, as the type of counseling mentioned earlier, may lead Catholics to seek a priest for sacramental confession, an experience that a number of times I have seen as the joyful outcome of our interaction.

On occasion, we find persons who have been away from the Church for some time and question sacramental confession. They may tell us that their non-Catholic Christian friends do not do it and quote the scribes' words in Mark 2:7, when Jesus forgives the paralytic's sins, "Who can forgive sins but God alone?" As Catholics, we cannot just avoid the issue once it has been brought up. I try to briefly explain to them that Jesus gave the authority he had to forgive sins as the Son of God to his apostles by saying, "Whatever you bind on earth shall be bound in heaven, and whatever you lose on earth shall be loosed in heaven" (Mt 16:19, NKJ). He also said to them after his resurrection, "Receive the Holy Spirit. If you forgive the sins of any, they are forgiven them; if you retain the sins of any, they are retained" (Jn 20:22–23, NKJ).[41]

Some patients express the desire to receive communion, but perhaps add that they have been away from the Church for a long time. I advise that a priest would be glad to visit them for confession. It gives me much happiness to see their joy at having been reconciled to God and the Church through the sacraments of reconciliation and communion. Often they agree with me when I ask them, "Wasn't your stay in the hospital worthwhile?"

Chapter 6 · Encountering the Problems: Physical and Spiritual

He will be with you, he will not leave you nor forsake you;
do not fear nor be dismayed (Dt 31:8, NKJ)

1. "I never prayed before"

We soon learn to see the hospital as a cauldron of many lives, reflecting many happy, unhappy and even broken homes, and teeming with spiritual problems that require much inner healing. Sometimes the person with whom we are about to pray makes the candid and painful confession, "I never prayed before."

It is heartbreaking, and reminds me of Clara, a student at a university in Hungary, who told me she had never prayed and asked, "How do you pray?" In situations like this, it can be helpful to say something like this:

> Jesus loves you very much. He is eager for you to seek him.
> That is why he gives you opportunities like this one. He will

give you more if you desire them in your heart, because he is telling you this right now: "Behold, I stand at the door [of your heart] and knock. If anyone hears my voice and opens the door, I will come in to him and dine with him and he with me" (Rv 3:20). You can do just that, open your heart, if you just talk to him as plainly as you are talking to me, right now or later in your room. Do not look for fancy words, just verbalize what you feel, as you would with your best friend; tell him that you are sorry you did not try a little harder to communicate with him before. Try, and you will see that you will feel his presence in your heart, speaking back to you.

I also remind patients that Jesus gave us the best prayer, and invite them to say the Our Father with me, slowly listening to every word. Then I paraphrase and explain each part briefly, suggesting that, from then on, besides praying those words, they begin to address him as they would their best friend, for they will discover that they are talking to someone who listens and likes to dialogue in our heart.

2. Why is there so much senseless suffering in the world?

The person who does not know God personally, nor understands his Son's sacrifice on the cross through a personal encounter with Jesus, runs the risk of forming torturous questions regarding suffering. Sometimes they even develop a hard cynicism, nurtured daily by images of suffering on television, in the press, and all around. This will surface as soon as we try to speak of God with them. They either blame God for their suffering or tacitly deny his existence. "Nothing makes any sense!" they often tell us. We cannot ignore the cry that comes from their hearts.

In the first place, much of the suffering around us does make sense, for it is caused by the many sins of the world. We tamper with God's creation, destroying resources (burning much-needed forests), polluting the sea (the mercury contamination of fish eaten by people on the Japanese island of Minimata that caused terrible defects and illness) and air (chemicals that destroy the ozone layer). The hatred between ethnic and religious groups generates devastating wars that cause the death of both the haters and the innocent. Excess indulgence in drugs, drinking, or smoking abuses and destroys our bodies. All of these and more produce chain reactions of suffering that spread from individual victims to families to groups to whole nations and down generations, dragging along countless innocent victims. We can say with John Paul II:

> The second half of our century—as if proportionally to the errors and transgressions of our contemporary civilization—carries such a terrible threat of nuclear war that we cannot think of this period but in terms of an incomparable accumulation of sufferings.[42]

At the same time, suffering is cradled by God's love for humanity. Although it is "a consequence of original sin, it acquires a new meaning as a participation in the saving work of Jesus (*CCC*, #1521), thanks to his own suffering and death on the cross for each and every one of us. Blessed Faustina, while praying for the suffering children in her native war-torn Poland, saw the Lord Jesus. "His eyes filled with tears, and he said to me, 'You see, my daughter, what great compassion I have for them. Know that it is they who uphold the world.'"[43]

Each person we visit is at a different stage in the journey toward God and the knowledge of him. Even Job, who personifies the quest for the answer to the questions "Why suffering?" and "Why do I suffer?" had not reached spiritual maturity until, having suffered much, he was able to confess, "I had heard of you by word of mouth, but now my eye has seen you. Therefore I disown what I have said, and repent" (Jb 42:5–6, NAB). We can always pray that this will happen to those we ourselves may never reach, because of their despondent and embittered attitude toward God whom they blame for their suffering.

To ask is always legitimate. As John Paul II tells us, "God expects the question and listens to it,"[44] as we see in the book of Job. Job saw himself innocent, yet suffering. Why? Because of sin? No, we do not suffer because of our sin, as his friends thought. The book of Job is like a prologue to the Christian response to suffering, reflecting Jesus' suffering. Yet, even in the Old Testament we see God punishing his people with a suffering which is truly a "merciful correction":

> Now I beg those who read this book not to be disheartened by these misfortunes, but to consider that these chastisements were meant for the correction of our nation. It is, in fact, a sign of great kindness to punish sinners promptly instead of letting them go for long (2 Mac 6:12–13).

God, just God that he is, may lovingly bring us to a crisis in our life to make us know his great love, just as he protects us from temptations and difficult situations. Sometimes we think we are seeking God when really he is seeking us. We must strive to show others that God truly works through the suffering he allows in our lives. We hope that, as Ralph Martin writes:

> All suffering can work to produce a clear understanding of what is important. It can help us keep our priorities clear. It can produce confidence in God rather than in ourselves, humbling us, showing us our limits and weaknesses, convincing us of how much we need power from on high and help from God.[45]

Do we have difficulty accepting that our physical or emotional suffering might be part of God's plan? A doctor prescribes painful therapy and we trust him or her and do it willingly. But if God, in his infinite wisdom and as part of his plan for us, provides spiritual therapy through trials and suffering, we cannot bear it.

> It hurts to stretch atrophied muscles, and it hurts to widen shrunken and stony hearts so that they can give and receive

> more love. Becoming holy is an often-excruciating process of rehabilitation....He knows what needs to be purified in us and how much pressure needs to be applied.[46]

Once we discover what it is all about, we can, while still experiencing a trial, "even boast of our affliction" (Rom 5:3, NAB), for we can recognize God's purpose: "See, I have refined you like silver, tested you in the furnace of affliction" (Is 48:10, NAB). Of one thing we can be sure: if our doctor knows our body better than we do, God certainly knows our whole being, body, mind, and spirit, infinitely better. We must try to reassure our suffering brothers and sisters by praying with them, asking for that grace won by Jesus on the cross by which we can overcome, if not the physical or emotional pain, then the sense of pointlessness and, above all, self-pity. How hard it is to minister to those who have abandoned themselves to it, enveloped by a thick veil through which God's light through us can hardly penetrate.

Sometimes we see suffering persons who see God's disciplining but loving hand, but many others fail to comprehend how they could derive any good fruit from their suffering. Yet, they might still have enough faith—and we should help them in this—to believe God when he tells us, "My thoughts are not your thoughts, nor are your ways my ways" (Is 55:8, NAB). At other times, we may be at a loss for words, almost afraid, as if we could hear God's admonition: "Who is this that obscures divine plans with words of ignorance?...Where were you when I founded the earth?" (Jb 38:2, 4, NAB).

It is the sin of the world, not our personal sin that God chastises. Moreover, when I join the sin of the world with my own sin, I may even lead others to sin in an endless chain reaction, a poison, transmitted from one to another, whose origin is ultimately in original sin.

But God the Father, creator of the universe, gave us the Son, Jesus, who, with the strength of the Holy Spirit, gave himself on the cross to offer us the opportunity to free ourselves. When we suffer we must remember his suffering and death as part of his Father's plan, a plan he knew and accepted. He ordered Peter to control himself during his arrest, for "how would the scriptures be fulfilled which say that it must come to pass in this way?" (Mt 26:54, NAB). Yet, he agonized over it, crying out to God, "My Father, if it is possible, let this cup pass from me; yet, not as I will, but as you will" (Mt 26:39, NAB). How well he knew the scriptures, how he must have thought of Isaiah's words during his passion:

> But he was pierced for our offenses, crushed for our sins, upon him was the chastisement that makes us whole, by his stripes we were healed....The Lord laid upon him the guilt of us all....Like a lamb led to the slaughter... (Is 53:5-7, NAB).

The passion of Jesus gives us the opportunity to put our sufferings to good use, overcoming any sense of pointlessness. It enables us to offer it to him and intercede for others. As John Paul II explains, if we do that, our suffering will become "creative" because we will turn it into something good, thus confirming that "all things works for good for those who love God" (Rom 8:28, NAB). That suffering, as he says, can be the beginning of our glory in heaven when we participate in the suffering of Jesus, for, as St. Paul writes:[47]

> We are children of God, and if children, then heirs, heirs of God and joint heirs with Christ, if only we suffer with him so that we may also be glorified with him...[for] the sufferings of this present time are as nothing compared with the glory to be revealed for us (Rom 8:16-18, NAB).

In these words, we see the relationship between suffering and holiness: glory implies "holiness." When I know a person's attitude toward God and pray holding his or her hand, I feel a profound reverence because I know that it is as if the three of us, Jesus, the sick person, and I, were holding hands while gathered together in his name (Mt 18:20). At a moment like that, I feel so small and insignificant, for I know that God is telling that person, "My grace is sufficient for you, for strength is made perfect in weakness" (2 Cor 12:9, NAB).

When Donna was given an injection for pain, I held her hand to help her feel Jesus' presence more tangibly as I prayed, because she was being pierced by pain at short intervals. Every time it came, she would squeeze my hand. She said, "Thank you! He is so good! He always comes when I need him!"

More and more, when I am with a terminally ill brother or sister I am in awe. I know that I am looking at a person who is so close to encountering God, meeting our loving Jesus at the very end of God's plan for him or her in this world, and about to pass into eternity, which Jesus won for us on the cross and to which we are a little closer every day. Like Harry, a very dear friend who said to us with glowing face, "I can't wait to meet my creator! I just can't wait to go through that door!"

Yet, as Raniero Cantalamessa, the preacher to the pope's household, tells us, we avoid the issue of eternity and do not even hear sermons on it, because secularism, which he defines as "forgetting...the eternal destiny of the human race...concentrating exclusively on...time present and on this world..." is "the most widespread and most insidious heresy of the modern age."[48] It takes our mind from God's eternal plan and prevents us from coping with suffering in a Christian way. Ralph Martin writes:

> Loyalty to God necessarily means purging evil from our own lives.... I've found it very helpful...to eliminate a lot of popular music, television, magazines and secular movies which don't help to accomplish our goal of following Christ with undivided loyalty. Being exposed to a lot of current popular entertainment inevitably weakens our desire to follow Christ, dulls our thirst for prayer, and lulls us into accepting immorality as normal and "not so bad."[49]

Who wants to think of eternal life when life here and now is so good! It is not easy to dwell on the thought of eternity without fear of losing everything unless we ask God to give us insight into his plan for us. For this we need the fellowship of Christian brothers and sisters, familiarity with his word, and spiritual literature until even when we suffer, we acquire the God-given certitude that "this momentary light affliction is producing for us an eternal weight of glory beyond all comparison" (2 Cor 4:17, NAB).

3. Personal hopelessness

The feeling of senselessness in the person who, lacking a sound spiritual formation, is unable to comprehend the reasons for the existence of suffering, results in an even worse sense of personal hopelessness. That person, seeing his or her sin without knowing God's constant offer of forgiveness for those who repent, no matter their past, inevitably falls into a fearful state of spiritual hopelessness that can be masked with cynicism, a dangerous armor we must try to break through for the sake of that person's spiritual and physical health. We must know what the Bible says about God's unconditional forgiveness if we repent, and try to transmit God's love as he did through Ezekiel:

> But if the wicked man turns away from all the sins he committed, if he keeps all my statutes and does what is right and just, he shall surely live, he shall not die. None of the crimes he committed shall be remembered against him....Do I indeed derive any pleasure from the death of the wicked?... Do I not rather rejoice when he turns from his evil way that he may live? (Ez 18:21–23, NAB)

Jesus expresses that joy of God when he tells us about the lost sheep in Luke 15:7, that "there will be more joy in heaven over a sinner who repents than over ninety-nine righteous people who have no need of repentance" (NAB).

4. Lost faith

If St. Paul confirms our tripartite nature when he expresses his good wishes for the Thessalonians' "spirit, soul, and body" (1 Thes 5:23, NAB), it follows that if any part suffers, the others suffer as well. Thus, when the body suffers, both the mind and the spirit may weaken, particularly when they have not been fortified by faith and trust in God. Not everybody can endure suffering and remain spiritual. Even Job was driven to despair when God allowed Satan to test him to the limit. We sometimes find people who, not having had a strong spiritual foundation, have lost their faith, or what little they had, and cannot bother with God.

Craig was a very young man with whom I talked for an hour after he admitted losing his faith because of the serious health problems he had endured since the age of sixteen. I spoke to him about what the Bible says concerning suffering, and he began to feel better. Then I laid hands on a gangrenous wound in his leg that had been paining him for some time. Later he told me the pain had ceased, and that the doctors were very pleased at his speedy recovery. I lent him a few books that he read avidly and passed on to his mother. The story of his life began to unfold and things to pray for were identified. I lent him a book on the sacraments, and he soon received the sacrament of reconciliation for the first time. He said he "felt great" and began to think of being confirmed, so I referred him to a priest. He began to come to Sunday mass with us, learned the main prayers, and never ceased to thank God for his recovery and newly-found faith. I even found him on his knees praying the rosary, after my co-worker Alex gave him a rosary and a book by St. Louis de Montfort. I hope his faith has continued to grow and that he did not return to his former darkness.

5. Estrangement from the Church

Estrangement from the Church often derives from a sinful situation or lifestyle, together with loss of faith. As time goes by I meet more and more persons who explain that they have not been to Church for quite some time. Without encouragement from me, they usually volunteer that confession with a sense of guilt. I try to explain how much better they would feel if they tried to return to the Church, and how they would profit from the sacraments. Often they say that they believe in God and pray, although they do not attend church. At times like this, we might recall Hebrews 10:25, "We should not stay away from our assembly, as is the custom of some" (NAB), remembering Paul's words: "So we are ambassadors for Christ, as if God were appealing through us. We implore you on behalf of Christ, be reconciled to God" (2 Cor 5:20, NAB).

Sandy, a pretty thirteen-year-old, candidly told me, "I don't go to church. I find it boring; the priest just tells jokes to make us laugh." For a few seconds I ached in silence. Once more I thought of the need to evangelize those who have only been "sacramental-ized," and of the "urgent need we have of an evangelization which is simple and essential, something attained by making Jesus Christ the initial and focal point of everything." I had just read those words in one of Fr. Cantalamessa's books, where he also says that today we run the risk of "spending most of the time taking care of the one sheep that remained in the sheepfold, instead of going after the ninety-nine strayed ones."[50]

I tried to explain to Sandy that I also found some priests boring, but that even if the priest doesn't do a better job, God is still in that church and Jesus shows his immense love for us and speaks to us in our hearts.

At other times, the estranged person may be in the last stages of a terminal illness. Like Vincent, in his early seventies, whom I visited even though he initially said, "Thank you, but I don't need anything." He told me he had been away from the Church for a long time. Seeing he was not happy about it, I told him he could always talk to a priest and asked if he would mind my praying for him. He accepted gratefully. I laid my hands on his and prayed. I thanked God for being faithful to his promise to be present whenever two or more gather in his name, acknowledged his love for "my brother Vincent" and asked him to fill his heart, mind, and body with his peace, which is already healing. He squeezed my hands and thanked me. Two weeks later, I prayed with him again, and again he was grateful. The following day he died.

6. Those bitter against God for their illness

"He gave me a kick in the rear," Floyd, a man with crippled legs, told me in the hospital. With bitter laughter, he had told me the same thing two years before. Then I had thought of Job's understandable despair, when he "cursed the day of his birth" (Jb 3:1, NKJ). I had tried to assure him of God's love and compassion. My wife and I had prayed for him for a while. This second time he was happy to see me and remembered things I had told him about God and about myself. Convinced of the injustice of his condition, his bitterness had kept him away from the Church for some years. This time, however, while telling me about a Spanish restaurant in Tampa, he suddenly changed the subject and said he would like to talk to a priest because he was thinking of coming back to the Church.

"Illness can lead to anguish, self-absorption, sometimes even despair and revolt against God." (*CCC*, #1501). Often, losing a weak faith is a direct consequence of blaming God for one's sickness and suffering. Personally, I find the embittered person very difficult to speak to. I can say what I want to say, but sometimes I hear my own words "as sounding brass or a clanging cymbal" (1 Cor 13:1, NKJ).

Although I remember that the cross of Christ is the answer to the mystery of suffering and that there are benefits of sharing in it with him through our own suffering, my own shortcomings often prevent me from knowing how to share with a pained, depressed, or angry person the words of St. Paul, "In my flesh I complete what is lacking in Christ's afflictions for the sake of his body, that is, the Church" (Col 1:24, RSV). To say at the wrong time that "in everything God works for good with those who love him" (Rom 8:28, RSV) may sound much like an accusation, as if I said, "You don't qualify for this promise." Many other times, however, I can see those very words touch the person's heart as a balm of hope. This thought gives me the strength to share what is in my heart instead of just listening to the person's complaint, remembering how it was precisely because of his own suffering that Job could discover God's majesty and confess in the end: "I had heard of thee by the hearing of the ear, but now my eye sees thee" (Jb 42:5, RSV).

When we have been able to establish a reasonable rapport, it can be surprisingly helpful to assure someone that it is only human to feel that way, even if our interaction at that point is more a monologue on our part.

7. Unforgiveness

Unforgiveness, if not dealt with, is a spiritual wound that keeps festering, no matter how much the person thinks the cause is forgotten or ignored. Benedict Groeschel reports having seen people debilitated by wounds of fifty years.[51] Its harmful effects are recognized even in secular contexts, as we read in *Time's* cover story on Pope John Paul II's forgiveness of his would-be assassin:

> Those who do not forgive are those who are less capable of changing the circumstances of their lives. Not to forgive is to be imprisoned by the past, by old grievances that do not permit life to proceed with new business. Not to forgive is to yield oneself to another's control. If one does not forgive, then one is controlled by the other's initiatives and is locked into sequence of act and response, of outrage and revenge, tit for tat, escalating always. The present is endlessly overwhelmed and devoured by the past. Forgiveness frees the forgiver. It extracts the forgiver from someone else's nightmare.[52]

As Christians, we know that God himself takes the burden off our shoulders when we have prayed for it and will grant us the grace of forgiving "seventy times seven" (Mt 18:22, NAB). Forgiving is the hardest thing asked of us, but in order that we might be able to forgive our worst enemies, "the love of God has been poured out into our hearts through the Holy Spirit that has been given to us" (Rom 5:5, NAB). Corrie ten Boom, concentration camp survivor, later met "one of the most cruel guards," who, not recognizing her, offered his hand and asked her to forgive him, since she had mentioned the camp.

> My blood seemed to freeze. But forgiveness was not an emotion. Forgiveness is an act of the will. "Jesus, help me!" [and she took his hand]. And then this healing warmth seemed to flood my whole being, bringing tears to my eyes. "I forgive you, brother!" I cried. "With all my heart." It was not my love. It was the power of the Holy Spirit, as recorded in Romans 5:5.

What Corrie ten Boom reports fits perfectly with the words from *Time:* Those who were able to forgive their former enemies were able also to return to the outside world and rebuild their lives, no matter what the physical scars. Those who nursed their bitterness remained invalids.[53]

The Romanian Evangelical pastor Richard Wurmbrand was tortured for fourteen years in the jails of his country, where

> the communists who had tortured us came to prison too, the tortured and the torturers in the same cell. And while the non-Christians showed hatred toward their former inquisitors and beat them, Christians took their defense giving away their last slice of bread (we had at that time one slice a week) and the medicine which could save their lives to a sick communist torturer, who was now a fellow prisoner.[54]

Many of us have not yet fully grasped the seriousness of God's commandment of forgiveness and the consequences of not obeying it: "If you do not forgive others, neither will your Father forgive your transgressions" (Mt 6:15, NAB). In fact, Jesus, on different occasions (e.g., the parable of the unforgiving servant, in Mt 18:21–35) would repeat what scripture had already stated:

> Forgive your neighbor the wrong he has done, and then your sins will be pardoned when you pray. Does a man harbor anger against another and yet seek for healing [or pardon] from the Lord? Remember the end of your life, and cease from enmity (Sir 28:2–3, 6).

There is one type of unforgiveness I encounter more than I would have thought. A Catholic woman had changed parishes after having been deeply hurt by her pastor. I told her she had lived with that unforgiveness for a long time and, although she said she had forgiven him, she had kept away from her parish for too long. I reflected with her on two things: that a priest is a human being, vulnerable to failure and in need of being forgiven by God daily; and that we must see Jesus in that minister. As St. Francis of Assisi wrote in his *Admonitions,*

> Even if they fall into sin, no one should pass judgment on them, for God has reserved judgment on them himself. They are in a privileged position because they have charge of the body and blood of our Lord Jesus Christ and so anyone who sins against them commits a greater crime than if he sinned against anyone else in the whole world.[55]

There is also a medical and pathological side to unforgiveness. This is documented throughout the Bible: "An evil spirit from God came over Saul" (1 Sm 18:10, NAB) when he was jealous of David; the psalmist warns, "Give up your anger, abandon your wrath;...it brings only harm" (Ps 37:8, NAB), while in Proverbs we are told that "Anxiety in a man's heart depresses it" (Prv 12:25, NAB), that "Jealousy rots the bones" (Prv 14:30, NAB) and "A depressed spirit dries up the bones" (Prv 17:22, NAB). Sirach advises us, "Drive resentment far away from you, for worry has brought death to many, nor is there aught to be gained from resentment. Envy and anger shorten one's life" (Sir 30:23, AB).

Christian Medical Foundation psychiatrist William Wilson describes a woman who suffered from incurable migraine head-aches for eight years and was unable to forgive her unfaithful hus-band. When, after much prayer with Dr. Wilson, she was finally able to forgive, she was totally healed.[56]

One of the most painful cases of unforgiveness I have encoun-tered was a young woman in Intensive Care who as soon as she opened her eyes told me: "I miss my sister...she was raped and murdered...she was strangled." I assured her that the Lord wanted to heal those memories and that she had to forgive her sister's killer because Jesus asks us to forgive our enemies. I prayed for her and gave her communion. The next day she was happy to see me, and again I talked to her and prayed. Another case was a woman in Psychiatry who told me she had not been able to forgive her mother since she was fifteen because she ridiculed her when she "refused to have sex with a boy because [I] thought it was wrong." After talking and praying she could say, "Yes, I have to forgive her; after all she's my mother. Thank you."

Sometimes we find patients who cannot forgive themselves. We should help them to reflect on the injustice they are doing them-selves, since God is willing to forgive them, and we should try to lead them, if they are Catholic, to the sacrament of reconciliation. Deep guilt for our past sins and our failure to seek God's forgiveness can lead to the kind of depression I recently saw in a middle-aged woman: "I cannot forgive myself for all the sins in my past life." I read to her a short prayer full of hope: "Remember no more the sins of my youth; remember me only in light of your love" (Ps 25:7, NAB), and prayed more or less like this:

> Father, my sister and I come before you to ask you to cleanse her mind and heart that through Christ we might be able to approach you as our loving Father. Show her that she needs to ask your forgiveness only once, for you have known her and loved her since before she was born, and that your Son Jesus is calling her into his arms and your Holy Spirit will fill her with your peace.

Finally, we must be aware of one frightening aspect of unforgiveness. Just as we can intercede for others with our prayer and fasting, and be God's channels of blessings for body, mind, and spirit, we can also affect them negatively by harboring and nurturing negative feelings such as resentment and anger, which are really curses. When we get hurt, the hurt easily generates anger, deep resentment sets in and, instead of responding as God commands us—"Bless those who persecute you, bless and do not curse them...Do not repay anyone evil for evil" (Rom 12:14, 17, NAB), "Do not return evil for evil, or insult for insult" (1 Pt 3:9, NAB)—we do the opposite, making that person our enemy. In Rev. George Kossicki's book on intercession, we read:

> We have a great power to curse and to bless, but most of us are unaware of this power. By our resentment, anger, criticism or negative feelings toward another...we in effect curse him and keep him bound—and ourselves as well....The power to bind and to loose (see Mt 16:19 and 18:18) accompanies the keys that are entrusted to the Church. Not only can we unlock, but unwittingly we can lock up and bind and not realize we are responsible. By our forgiveness, unbinding and blessing, we can even bring freedom to people at a distance.[57]

Chapter 7 ·
With Jesus Through
a Hospital

*In the time of their visitation
they will shine forth, and shall dart
about as sparks through stubble (Wis 3:7, NAB)*

1. Sadness, anxiety, and despondency

"Every illness can make us glimpse death" (*CCC*, #1500), and that invariably causes anxiety until we regain our peace through our faith and prayer. One can openly inquire about this problem. It may be apparent as soon as we meet the patients: in their voice, in their irregular breathing, in their lack of interest in reading, even in the absent way they watch television. If they mention the scheduled operation, the tests to be done, the awaited diagnosis, or the unknown cause of pain or general discomfort, there is a reason for us to pray for that situation.

It is good to ask, "Are you anxious?" or "How do you feel?" The patients may admit anxiety, as if seeking relief. Only a few say they're all right. Often we sense sadness, which stirs the love of

God in our hearts. It may be elicited by loneliness and alienation, or by a sense of loss. We must try to bring some joy to their minds. As St. Francis de Sales tells us, "Sadness, which is justified in the beginning, produces anxiety. Anxiety again produces an increase of sadness, and this is extremely dangerous."[58]

When this is the case, we are witnessing neither the sadness of compassion or of repentance. According to St. Francis, there are only two good kinds: "godly sorrow," as St. Paul calls it in 2 Corinthians 7:10, and what he calls "worldly sorrow," which "produces death" (NAB). "The enemy," St. Francis tells us, "makes use of sadness in order to practice his temptations on the just" and it "excites inordinate fears, creates a disgust for prayer, stupefies and oppresses the brain, deprives the mind of counsel, resolution, judgment, and courage." Alluding to James 5:10, he adds that "prayer is a sovereign remedy."[59] That is what we should try to do with patients, rebuking those spirits of sadness that keep them enslaved by asking God to deliver them in the name of his Son Jesus, praising and thanking him, and claiming his promise to those in exile, "I will turn their mourning into joy, I will console and gladden them after their sorrows" (Jer 31:13).

As for anxiety itself, at times blended with sadness, St. Francis de Sales assures us that it

> is the greatest evil that can befall the soul, sin only excepted....Anxiety proceeds from an inordinate desire of being delivered from the evil that we feel or of acquiring the good that we hope for. Yet there is nothing that tends more to increase evil and prevent the enjoyment of good than inquietude and anxiety.[60]

2. Fear

It is good to encourage those prone to be tempted by fear to call on the name of the Lord, for "The name of the Lord is a strong tower, the just man runs to it and is safe" (Prv 18:10, NAB).

When the enemy attacks, we should pray, "Lord Jesus, help me," or the ancient and powerful Jesus Prayer, "Lord Jesus Christ, Son of God, have mercy on me."

Dr. William Reed understands this very well:

> Fear, whether of death or illness, is a tool of Satan used to defeat Christians and to bring about all manner of illnesses and emotional problems. Fear activates the disease process as well as symptoms. The Holy Bible states, "There is no fear in love; but perfect love casteth out fear: because fear hath torment..." (1 Jn 4:18). God is love....the more fear we have, the less of God we have; the more of God we have, the less fear we have. Paul states in Romans 8:15, "For ye have not received the spirit of bondage again to fear; but ye have received the Spirit of adoption, whereby we cry, Abba Father."[61]

He also enlightens us concerning those patients who

> develop a morbid fear of their illness which paralyzes them from doing anything of a constructive nature with reference to their illness....Fear is perhaps the greatest ally of cancer and can only be removed from the person through an act of the will to do something about his illness and through the intervention of God in the total person of the individual—spirit, soul, and body. The Ministry of Healing should never be conducted apart from the doctor and the nurse.[62]

Reading what both a saint and a Christian physician have to say about fear should be enough for pastoral care visitors who have to try to deal with such an overwhelming emotion. If we are familiar with God's word and his faithfulness to it, we should be able to claim it when we remember the words that he gave us to say back to him,

He will never leave you, nor forsake you. So do not fear or be dismayed" (Dt 31:8).

O Lord, my rock, my fortress, my deliverer, my God, my rock of refuge! (2 Sm 22:2-3).

Be my rock of refuge, a stronghold to save me. You are my rock and my fortress (Ps 31:2-3/3-4).

I sought the Lord, who answered me, delivered me from all my fears (Ps 34:4/5).

When I am afraid, in you I place my trust (Ps 56:3/4).

Often, if I see signs of fear, I ask gently, "Are you afraid?" They sometimes answer yes, and I suggest we pray about that. I begin by praising and glorifying Jesus and thanking him because we know that if we are there together in his name, he is with us because He promises it. I might address the Father and claim, in the name of the Son, the promises just quoted, asking him to deliver them from the bondage of fear. For he sent Jesus "to proclaim liberty to captives" (Lk 4:18, NAB). We should always try to instill in the hearts and minds of our brothers and sisters the simple trust in God that St. Peter fostered among the early Christians, always exposed to persecution and violence: "Cast all your worries upon him because he cares for you" (1 Pt 5:7, NAB).

3. "I'm too old. What am I doing here?"

Some people, having reached a very advanced age, actually say this. I have an uncle who is 97. He often asks, "What am I doing here? I don't know why God keeps me here. It's about time he takes me." A very dear 96-year-old woman whom we have been seeing for over twenty years says: "I've been here long enough. Time to leave this country!" My uncle lives in a residence and our elderly friend lives in a room in a small rest home surrounded by other women who can hardly communicate.

77

Elderly people who live as part of a household, and enjoy the daily company of children and grandchildren seldom complain and wonder what they are doing in this life. When I talk to them I try to assure them that if God allows them to be here it is because he has a plan for each one of us, and knows and loves each one of us personally: "Before I formed you in the womb I knew you" (Jer 1:5, NAB). If we read his word, we will acknowledge his eternal knowledge of us when we tell him, "In your book they were all written; the days fashioned for me, when as yet there were none of them" (Ps 139:16, NKJ). We are told, "Look, as the clay is the potter's hand, so are you in my hand" (Jer 18:6, NKJ).

We must assure those who feel they have outlived their usefulness that, although they may not be doing the things they used to, they can serve God by praying for their dead and the sick, for those who do not have the faith they have, and for the many needs of the world, for God certainly hears their prayers. As Dr. Paul Tournier writes:

> What is important for the aged is not what they are still able to do, nor yet what they have accumulated and cannot take with them. It is what they are. This is the cause of the dreadful feeling of uselessness that so deeply bothers most elderly people....All that I can hope, when my time for action will be over, is that I may yet go further in the riches of this knowledge [of God].[63]

4. Visiting in Psychiatry

Although we in this ministry confront sin and darkness—for "our struggle is not with flesh and blood but with principalities, with the powers, with the world rulers of this present darkness, with the evil spirits in the heavens" (Eph 6:12, NAB), and how "the father of lies" (Jn 8:44, NAB) can sharpen our feelings and emotions when we are weakened by illness—we must avoid any tendency to interpret mental illness as the work of the devil.

Like any other unit in the hospital, Psychiatry is a place where, backed by prayer, with trust in God's love for our brothers and sisters and armed in our minds with "the sword of the Spirit, which is the word of God" (Eph 6:17, NAB), we can do much good, while being extremely careful not to interfere with the professionals as we talk to the patients. We should not overstay when visiting there, nor give anyone spiritual books, particularly anything concerning healing, as we might do them more harm than good. Let us remember, lest we should be tempted to abuse our prerogatives as pastoral care visitors, that the Lord can use all circumstances and people to accomplish his purposes, including nonbelieving but competent and compassionate professionals, just as we see in the Bible that sometimes God used even his people's enemies to help them.

We can use one of the many prayers of trust we find in scripture, for instance: "Incline your ear to me, make haste to rescue me! Be my rock of refuge, a stronghold to save me. You are my rock and my fortress, for your name's sake lead and guide me (Ps 31:2-3/3-4, NAB). One day the mass readings were all scriptural passages about hope and God's mercy. I took communion to a young woman who suffered from depression. I invited her to take her Bible and read Psalm 103 with me, from which I chose verses 1-3 (NAB), commenting on the concepts I emphasize here:

> Bless the Lord, my soul;/*all my being, bless* his holy name!/ Bless the Lord, my soul;/*do not forget all the gifts of God,/ Who pardons all your sins,/heals all your ills,/*Delivers your life from *the pit,*/surrounds you with love and compassion,/ Fills your days with good things;/*your youth is renewed* like the eagle's.

I gave her a copy of a picture of Jesus knocking on a house door, below which I had typed the words from Revelation 3:20. I also gave her a photograph of St. Thérèse of Lisieux, telling her what a wonderful intercessor that young saint is, and on its back I

79

wrote for her the following references for further reading: Psalm 34:17-19/18-20, Romans 5:3-5, Romans 8:28, 1 Corinthians 10:13, and Philippians 4:6-7. Our Bible, used wisely, can be a wonderful tool in pastoral care.

Since we often do not know exactly what to pray for, and we do not seek information—patients may not even be able to explain why they are there—we should just ask Jesus to fill their minds with his peace and defend them from anything that would not come from him. Those who can pray in tongues—a gift of the Spirit fruitfully renewed among many Christians today—can do so quietly, "For we do not know what to pray as we ought, but the Spirit himself intercedes" (Rom 8:26, NAB).

5. Visiting in Intensive Care

It is sad to see that some pastoral care visitors shrink from visiting in Intensive Care. These are the patients who need our prayer most, and if relatives are there, they may need our prayerful words of comfort as well. The hospital where I visit has a small lounge with a kitchenette where relatives may stay as long as they wish when they are not with the patient. There is enough privacy there to speak to them and suggest prayer. I have had beautiful experiences in Intensive Care, both in that lounge and in the unit itself, and I always found the patient's relatives most willing for me to lead them in prayer. Sometimes, if the relatives are from different religious denominations, praying with them is a very good opportunity for the sort of ecumenical contact discussed in Chapter 8. Since the chapel happens to be very close, I sometimes offer, if they are Catholics, to lead them in prayer before the Blessed Sacrament. Warm bonds are established in this type of interaction with relatives of the patients.

Inside the unit, new patients are asked whether they want to see us. When it is impossible to communicate with them, I just stand by the bedside and lay a hand on them or gently stroke their forehead while talking to them and praying softly, hoping they will hear what I am saying, and always knowing that the Lord is with them, that he loves them and hears our prayer. My words are not only of intercession, asking God in the name of Jesus to be with them, have mercy on them, protect them and touch them, but of encouragement, telling them I look forward to seeing them when they get better, to thank and praise God for their recovery. It is very important to intersperse our prayer with praise to the Father and Jesus, and ask them to join us in their hearts, sometimes quoting or reading from scripture:

> He will be with you and will never fail you or forsake you. So do not fear or be dismayed (Dt 31:8, NAB).

> I love you, Lord, my strength. Lord, my rock, my fortress, my deliverer. My God, my rock of refuge, my shield (Ps 18:2/3, NAB).

> Even when I walk through a dark valley, I fear no harm, for you are at my side (Ps 23:4, NAB).

> Have mercy on me, God, have mercy on me (Ps 57:1/2, NAB).

> You are my Father, my God, the rock that brings me victory (Ps 89:26/27, NAB).

> O Lord, my strength, my fortress, my refuge in the day of distress (Jer 16:19, NAB)

> Ah, Lord God, you have made heaven and earth by your great might....nothing is impossible to you (Jer 32:17, NAB).

One more thing to mention concerning Intensive Care is that we should be careful what we say in front of persons who are comatose or anesthetized. If those who are with them begin to speak inappropriately, we should not hesitate to courteously signal them to change the subject or keep quiet. Dr. William Reed states:

It is my considered opinion, after the observation of many anesthetized patients, that it is possible to implant negatives into the subconscious mind and conceivably into the spiritual being of the patient at the time of anesthesia or unconsciousness, which are of definitive bearing on the patient's postoperative course and on the total outcome of whatever procedure has been used to correct the abnormality....it is entirely possible for the patient to be adversely affected by those things which occur while he is not conscious.[64]

Barbara Shlemon also writes:

A person in a coma is often able to hear what is being said, even if unable to respond in a visible way....People who have survived comatose states will often be able to relate entire conversations which went on in their rooms....Many times such persons have related to me the tremendous effect the word of God had upon them in their helpless condition. One woman...declares, "I was given the courage to live when I heard my sister repeatedly saying 'I can do all things through Christ who strengthens me'" (43).[65]

Thus, we should never just leave the patient because we see that he is not conscious. Often I tell him that I will touch him with the body of Jesus (that is, with the pyx), that Jesus is with him because he loves him very much, that he should not be afraid because Jesus is with him every minute, working through the doctors and the nurses, and that he is going to be all right.

We must also remember that each of those visits in ICU may very well be—as happened my first time there—the last opportunity for a person to receive prayer, to hear of Jesus' love, and to be lifted up to God. We might even be the last ones to pray with that person before he or she dies, as happened with Alma, a middle-aged woman who had been removed from life support the second time I went to see her. I knew that Jesus had been very close to us.

6. The grieving patient

It is common for some patients to be in the hospital and at the same time grieving over the death of a close relative or friend. It is good to converse with them a little, even if they have told us that they will not be needing us, and to offer to pray for them. I have seen some obsessed by the loss of a daughter or son years before, showing a deep, gnawing wound that we know God wants to heal. Invariably, we find that the degree of their pain varies with the strength of their faith and trust in God. We will know when opening our Bible and reading it to them, or applying it to their situation in our own words, is going to help.

> But the souls of the just are in the hand of God, and no torment shall touch them....Chastised a little, they shall be greatly blessed, because God tried them and found them worthy of himself (Wis 3:1, 5, NAB).

> But I do not want you to be ignorant, brethren, concerning those who have fallen asleep, lest you sorrow as others do who have no hope. For if we believe that Jesus died and rose again, even so God will bring with him those who sleep in Jesus (1 Thes 4:13–14, NKJ).

> For I consider that sufferings of this present time are not worthy to be compared with the glory which shall be revealed in us (Rom 8:18, NKJ).

> "Therefore,[let us] console one another with these words" (1 Thes 4:18, AB).

7. Visiting in Maternity

I deliberately speak of visiting in Maternity and Pediatrics and then of death because they represent the two ends of our earthly existence and symbolize the span of a life, which is but "a vapor that appears briefly and then disappears" (Jas 4:14, NKJ).

At first I was not too excited about visiting that unit of the hospital, but then I began to see God's wonderful mystery of life in the infant with the mother or both parents, or in the pregnant woman, when sometimes I ask her to put my pyx to her abdomen while I pray for the child and read Psalm 139:13–16, slowly, letting them savor every word:

> You formed my inmost being; you knit me in my mother's womb. I praise you, so wonderfully you made me; wonderful are your works! My very self you knew; my bones were not hidden from you, when I was being made in secret, fashioned as in the depths of the earth. Your eyes foresaw my actions; in your book all are written down; my days were shaped, before one came to be (NAB).

Recently as I heard a child's beating heart through the ultrasound machine, I thought of when Elizabeth's "infant leaped in her womb" (Lk 1:41, NAB). Often the new mother cries from joy while the father, eyes glistening, hands her a tissue. Sometimes I also read Hannah's words of consecration of Samuel to God:

> "For this child I prayed, and the Lord has granted me my petition which I asked of him. Therefore I also have lent him to the Lord; as long as he lives he shall be lent to the Lord." So they worshiped the Lord there (1 Sm 1:27–28, NKJ).

We are helping parents to acknowledge that gift from God that belongs to him and they must offer to him so that his will be done in his or her life. My prayer for the baby, while touching them with the pyx, will be something like this:

> And, Lord, protect him/her. Bless each day in his/her life and give him/her the opportunity to get to know you in a personal way as his/her savior. We thank you, Lord, for____, part of your people. May he/she be always faithful to you as you are faithful to him/her. As his/her mother

receives your body, Lord, touch also the body of this child, which is her own body.

I also find in Maternity mothers who think they are all right and do not need anything. I leave, of course, but not without reminding them that the fact that everything went well is reason to thank God. Occasionally, when I sense openness, I also read from Psalm 139; and even if they do not want anything else, they love it and tears come to their eyes. That is also evangelization, a little seed we are supposed to plant, leaving its watering up to the Lord.

Once in a while I meet a very young unwed mother, to whom I again enjoy reading those four verses of Psalm 139 in a special way, pondering with her how other sons or daughters like hers are being killed by abortion. When I pray, I thank God for the love he put in her heart for her child and lift up to the Lord those who may be contemplating abortion, that, through the intercession of Mary, Mother of all, they may change their minds. This interaction sometimes may lead them to share their desire to have their baby baptized and, on occasion, even to get married in the Church. Although I immediately suggest that they speak to a priest—and I may get in touch with the pastor of their own parish—I often need to answer some basic questions they have regarding baptism, marriage, and the like. Again, we find ourselves in a position to conduct preliminary counseling—thanks to which we will call a priest—clearly stating the position of the Church.

8. Visiting in Pediatrics

In the hospital where I visit, only a glass door separates Pediatrics and the Palliative Care unit: the sick children on one side, the older, very ill and dying on the other. Until recently, I have found it more difficult to visit the children than the terminally ill patients. One of the reasons is that the young parents are often the ones who say, "We are all right, thank you," unfortunately reflecting the attitude of so many young people today. There are also times when one senses the anxiety of those parents and their need to be prayed with, along with the child. They usually accept our offer with gratitude if approached with sensitivity, and occasionally will ask themselves. Here we can always pray knowing Jesus' great love for that child, putting him or her in Jesus' arms, asking his Mother Mary to show her love for that mother and her child.

I like to apply the pyx to the child's body while I pray, imagining the body of Jesus touching it, and just thank and praise him for it. I did that to a very small girl who was extremely restless, crying and writhing in her mother's arms, making it difficult for her parents to concentrate on my prayer. She stopped instantly. I calmly repeated "Thank you, Jesus; thank you, Jesus; touch her, Jesus, touch her; thank you, Jesus; praise you, Jesus," quite a few times. She remained quiet and I left the room.

9. Terminal illness and expected death

At times, we confront the worst: the dying patient and the somber attitude of impending death. Our heart goes to them and we would like to help them, particularly if we see they are willing to talk or pray. It is the time when they need our comfort. How much comfort we can offer depends first on the person's faith, and then on how grounded our own words are on God's own word. We may paraphrase it or quote it, but it must be communicated to that brother or sister, since it will be the only one truly "piercing to the division of soul and spirit" (Heb 4:12, NKJ).

How much love we need to ask God to put in our hearts for those who are dying and how our hearts go out to them! We visit with them, pray with them, hold their hands, sometimes even receive their loving embrace when we grow very close to each other. But there are also times when we instinctively tend to make that visit shorter because we want to escape from pain. It is hard to face someone who knows that we know death is approaching, who is already closer to God's judgment than to this world. Yet, I have come to appreciate precisely that as a privilege, realizing that I am talking to someone who will meet Jesus soon and will be able to intercede for me before the throne of God. Although I always approach a dying patient with deep respect, regardless of his or her attitude, I must confess that I relate much better to a Christian. In fact, my wife and I have been immensely uplifted and have always received some healing of our own human fear of death when we have been with someone who either is able to face it with faith and trust without the slightest attitude of rebellion but with peaceful acceptance of God's will, or whose trust in the Lord is so deep that their faces glow in anticipation, as if they were about to be married. Their souls seem to burn within them for their union with their bridegroom:

> Behold, he stands behind our wall; he is looking through the windows, gazing through the lattice (Sg 2:9, NKJ).

Many years ago, a Canadian community of Spanish nuns offered my friend and me a joyful meal. Two weeks later we visited one of the sisters, who was dying of cancer in a hospital. At that time, I marveled at what she said to us with a smile: "Jesus is waiting for me!"

In the spring of 1997, we were visiting our very dear friend Harry, whom I mentioned earlier. Through the years, he lovingly shared with us his deep love for the Lord, his vast knowledge of scripture, and, together with his wife, Elaine, his prayer. Although already quite debilitated by cancer, he received a real healing after we and later a group of Pentecostal friends prayed with him. For two months he enjoyed wood chopping, snowplowing, and working on a car for many hours, and was eating well. Then, after that "bonus from the Lord," as he and his wife called it, he knew he was going to die. I quote again what he said to us with the glowing smile he always had when talking about the things of God: "I can't wait to meet my creator! I just can't wait to go through that door!"

My beloved spoke, and said to me: "Rise up, my love, my fair one, and come away. For, lo, the winter is past" (Sg 2:10, NKJ).

Another death my wife and I will never forget was that of Sana, the beautiful 24-year-old daughter of a Lebanese family, who died in our hospital after suffering for four years with a brain infection that rendered her totally unresponsive during her last two months. Even during the weeks when she could not even open her eyes anymore, seeing her peaceful expression was seeing Jesus, whom she radiated. His love filled the room, and her parents, Gebrael and Samira, who stayed with her day and night for nine weeks, were a powerful example of love and the acceptance of God's will. When she died, she was dressed as a bride and at her funeral a nuptial march played softly. Her parents were shattered, but "the peace of God that surpasses all understanding" (Phil 4:7, NKJ) reigned in their home above their excruciating pain.

I have not had occasion to face this situation with an unbelieving family, since they do not generally request the services of clergy or other pastoral care workers. But in all other instances, in my prayer for the dying person or in speaking to the relatives, I try to assure them that God is in control and that we Christians believe all of his promises of eternal life and accept his will, knowing that God has been joining that suffering to the suffering of his Son Jesus on the cross for their relative and for each one of us. They always appreciate hearing God's words at that time.

10. Praying for healing?

We know that "Jesus Christ is the same yesterday, today, and forever" (Heb 13:8, NAB). He says he is among us "to heal the brokenhearted" (Lk 4:18, NKJ). Just as "they brought to him all sick people who were afflicted with various diseases and torments, and those who were demon-possessed, epileptics and paralytics; and he healed them" (Mt 4:24, NKJ), so he also instructs us, "Heal the sick, cleanse the leper, raise the dead, cast out demons. Freely you have received, freely give" (Mt 10:8, NKJ). We should "lay hands on the sick, and they will recover" (Mk 16:18, NAB). Thus, most times I just obey that command, leaving the results to him.

We also know that he has always worked extraordinary healings and miracles through the saints and through many other holy Christians, as well as through ordinary and humble people who love God because they know that he is loving and faithful and fulfills his promises. Today Jesus continues to work all kinds of signs and wonders in our midst, healing people physically, emotionally, and spiritually, multiplying food and working extraordinary conversions through the power of his Holy Spirit in those who trust in his promises.

I have learned about some specific miracles from the personal testimonies of the poor Mexican brothers and sisters who live in Juárez with Jesuit Rev. Rick Thomas and Sr. Linda Koontz, S.N.J.M., and those of physicians within the interdenominational Christian Medical Foundation (United States and Canada), Caring Professions Concern (England), and Association of Christian Therapists (United States). On the other hand, Catholics and many non-Catholics experience healings and profound conversions during visits to famous Marian shrines such as Medjugorje (which I visited twice and witnessed the centrality of Jesus) and Lourdes, because Jesus' Mother still intercedes for us as she first did at Cana. There is today much faith-building literature on Christian healing, worked by God through priests, religious, pastors, and many Spirit-filled lay people in all Christian Churches.

Who is to pray for healing, when and with whom, in our pastoral care ministry? We need discernment, which God will give to us in direct proportion to the depth of our spiritual life and according to the degree in which we surrender to him, knowing that we are all sinners and that only with his grace can we be channels of his peace, his Word, and his loving healing.

In 1978, I spent a month in the hospital. Next door to me was Ray, a lovable 81-year-old man with cancer of the throat. Not being able to swallow even water, he was fed intravenously. I will never forget his longing for a hot cup of tea. He also suffered terribly from asthma, which was not helped by a medicated aerosol he received every four hours. When I became a Canadian citizen in 1976, the judge gave me a New Testament, and I was reading it seriously for the first time during that God-given stay in the hospital. Jesus' promises attracted me the most: "They will lay hands on the sick, and they will recover" (Mk 16:18, NKJ), "Ask, and it will be given to you; seek, and you will find" (Mt 7:7, NAB), "Whatever you ask in prayer, believing, you will receive" (Mt 21:22, NKJ). I was also drawn by the testimonies I kept finding in Acts, when Jesus was still so fresh in the minds and hearts of these first Christians. The year before I had read the now classic *Healing* by the Catholic Francis MacNutt,[66] and the books of the late Episcopalian Agnes Sanford.[67] It all sounded so logical to me and Jesus was becoming so real in my heart that, like Job, I was beginning to see Jesus with my own eyes, certainly with the eyes of my heart.

One night, when everything was quiet on the floor and Ray slept, I slipped into his room and laid my hands on his heaving chest and prayed: "Lord, I know he is going to die, but if he could only breath normally! Please, Lord, help him to breath." I then returned to my room. The following morning, when I asked the nurses about Ray, one answered, "Well, at least he doesn't need the aerosol anymore!" That did something to me. When I left the hospital, I kept visiting Ray every day, but in August, my wife and I were going to a charismatic conference in South Bend, Indiana. I went to say goodbye to Ray, and, still pained by his simple desire for a hot cup of tea, I uttered another simple prayer: "Lord, I know he is dying, but if he could at least swallow his cup of tea, Lord...Please, Lord?" When we came back I found him having his cup of tea, and for the last ten days before he died, not only did he swallow his cup of tea, but the biscuits I dipped in it too!

One does not always pray for the big things. Basic discernment hopefully guides us when we interact with the sick, and when I do, sometimes I am too shy to share that prayer with the patient because of my own sinfulness. It still robs me of the freedom I should have in my relationship with God, because I still need much healing myself in order to become a clean vessel of intercession. I have no doubt whatsoever that the Lord can heal a dying patient because "for God all things are possible" (Mt 19:26, NAB). I received a dramatic healing from asthma, when at the 1984 Christian Medical Foundation conference, where doctors shared many testimonies of healings, Dr. Reed prayed for me. I have seen countless proofs of physical and emotional healing in different Christian Churches. However, I never fail to ask the Lord to give the person his peace. All pastoral care visitors should pray for this, particularly when they see that peace is lacking. I remember Dr. Reed saying, "I never pronounce a case incurable until I see the person dead."

And yet, most of us are afraid to lay hands and pray for healing, even when interceding at a distance. Once at mass they read the following prayer of intercession for a terminally ill priest (to whom I had been privileged to minister in the hospital two years earlier): "...that God will help him to overcome fear, loneliness, and anxiety." That wording saddened me, for I felt it should have been more like, "Father, in the name of your Son Jesus Christ we ask you *to prevent* any feeling of fear, loneliness, or anxiety to come to our brother. And, Lord, we your people ask you to heal him, for your glory." He was terminally ill, but I could not help remembering how in 1961 in the city of Fredericton, the Rev. Bill Drost (later a gifted Spirit-filled Pentecostal pastor in Colombia and Spain) was healed in a few days by his prayers and those of his congregation when he was dying of a metastasized abdominal cancer.

I would like to close this chapter by quoting from a 1995 letter from Dr. Reed, in which he updated me on his brother-in-law's healing (reported earlier in the CMF bulletin) when, immediately after being taken off his life support, Dr. Reed and the patient's son laid hands on him and began to pray.

> It really is amazing that he was supposed to die but actually when the life support system was discontinued, he began immediately to get well....I feel that when we pray something always happens to the person we pray for spiritually, that is to say, on the level of the spirit and that this healing gradually goes through into the psychosoma.

Chapter 8 ·
Praying with Our
Brothers and Sisters

Learn to savor how good the Lord is;
happy are those who take refuge in
him (Ps 34:8/9, NAB)

1. Our own prayer habits

As a Catholic I always think that, as members of the Church originally founded by Jesus through Peter, we have a tradition of prayer, carried out through the centuries by the saints, by monastic and other religious communities, and by the faithful themselves. We possess a treasury of written prayers, beginning with the mass, many of them attributed to the saints, which we will always cherish as part of our heritage.

However, despite a wealth of Catholic writings on spontaneous vocal prayer, as well as on mental and contemplative prayer, the majority of us, particularly in the presence of one another, favor formal prayer—besides the centuries-old rosary, centered mostly on Jesus' life and passion—over the kind of Spirit-led spontaneous prayer, more common among many non-Catholics. Some portions of the Catholic Church, most characteristically within the Charismatic Renewal, have been reaching a balance between both types in the last decades. Bishops and priests, religious, and the laity offer testimonies about their enriched prayer life and their growth in spontaneous prayer in the freedom of the Spirit, as well as in praying in tongues (1 Cor 12:10, 14:2, 5, 14:18), all of which can be witnessed at large charismatic Catholic and ecumenical gatherings.

Spontaneous vocal prayer—without neglecting the most important formal prayers—gives a new dimension to our prayer experience and deepens our personal spiritual life and that of the community. In pastoral care, it allows us to express ourselves according to need as the Spirit leads us, and the patients appreciate our "personalized" prayer, often experiencing its therapeutic effect in different ways.

2. The prayer of praise

"His praise shall continually be in my mouth" (Ps 34:1/2, NKJ), "My mouth shall be filled with your praise, shall sing your glory every day" (Ps 71:8, NAB), we read in the Bible. Yet one aspect of prayer that tends to be neglected by Catholics is the prayer of praise, just praising God for who he is. God tells us: "Those who offer praise as a sacrifice honor me" (Ps 50:23, NAB). The Bible is full of exhortations to praise: "It is good to sing praises to our God (Ps 147:1, NKJ), "Daily he shall be praised" (Ps 72:15, NKJ), and we proclaim, "You are holy, who inhabit the praises of Israel" (Ps 22:3, NKJ). That is why we must "continually offer the sacrifice of praise to God, that is, the fruit of our lips" (Heb 13:15, NKJ).

Amazingly, while praise is the most important form of prayer in many Churches, Catholics do not realize that the history of their Church abounds precisely in established praises, conspicuously in the mass: the Alleluia; the Gloria; the "Glory to you, Lord Jesus Christ" after the gospel; the Acclamation "Holy, Holy, Holy..."

before the Eucharistic Prayer. Even in the Lord's Prayer, Jesus gave us praise to his Father. The majority of priests and their congregations seem to recite them by rote and with a demeanor that could never suggest joyful praise, whereas in some sectors of the Catholic Church and other churches people spend much time in praise because they know that God truly dwells in their praises, as his word says. Praise is the most important kind of prayer, through which God can act, even before we ask anything. I like to quietly but audibly praise Jesus during my prayer right after I give his body to patients. We must foster praise, sometimes explaining why we do it:

> We thank you, Lord, for your presence with us and we praise you because we know that you want our praise above all other kinds of prayer, and that you are already responding to our prayer when we praise you.

Recently I heard the disconsolate crying of a woman in her late sixties confined to a wheelchair due to very severe arthritis. She was moaning, crying, aching in her heart so much that I held her hands and began to stroke her head, alternatively praying for her and telling her how much Jesus loved her. I noticed her rosary, told her that Mary loved her too, and prayed for her and invited her to just praise Jesus and talk to him, which she immediately did, asking forgiveness for her sins. She talked about seeing a priest and asked me to give her communion, which she had not previously requested. Praying for whatever memories she had to heal, and again praising God the Father and Jesus, I quoted the words of the gospel of that day's mass, John 3:16, "For God so loved the world that he gave his only Son" (NAB). She was calm and happy when I left.

My wife, María, due to a spell of poor health, gradually sunk into a deep state of fatigue and depression. Late one afternoon, she could not drag herself out of bed to prepare dinner. She had two phone calls: first, from a member of an Anglican prayer group, who had not meant to dial our number, but promised to call their prayer chain; then from a member of the Hispanic prayer group who encouraged her to just praise the Lord, which María began to do continuously, feeling his peace take possession of her, until she could in fact cook a great dinner!

3. The prayer of thanks

We know that of the ten lepers Jesus healed, as related in Luke 17:11–19, only one "returned, glorifying God in a loud voice; and he fell at the feet of Jesus and thanked him" (NAB). We see many who, like the nine other lepers, do not seem to feel the need to thank God for their recovery and refer only to the medical staff or to their good luck. Many of those who request our prayers are not as eager to offer thanks as they were to petition. Yet, the psalmist acknowledges "Even before a word is on my tongue, Lord, you know it all" (Ps 139:4, NAB), and Jesus himself assures us, "Your Father knows what you need before you ask him" (Mt 6:8, NAB). It is true that Jesus also tells us to ask, "For everyone who asks, receives" (Lk 11:10, NAB), but Paul reminds us in Ephesians 5:20 that, above all, we should be "giving thanks always and for everything in the name of our Lord Jesus Christ to God the Father" (NAB). Very often, I have to say to a patient who is recovering and no longer seems to need us, "We shouldn't take it for granted; that is something to thank God for." The Lutheran pastor and theologian Dietrich Bonhoeffer wrote:

> Only he who gives thanks for little things receives the big things. We prevent God from giving us the great spiritual gifts he has in store for us, because we do not give thanks for daily gifts.[68]

The other prayer of thanks, which is even more important, is when we praise God the Father or Jesus not for what we have visibly received, but for his love, his mercy, his faithfulness, his protection, his presence, and, certainly, for the very fact that he allows us to receive the medical care we take so for granted, while so many in the world suffer and die for want of it. When I see patients with their tray of food, I sometimes ask, "May I say grace with you?" As for the Christian habit of saying grace, I remind them that Jesus blessed food before eating (Mt 26:26) and that the first letter to Timothy speaks of "foods that God created to be received with thanksgiving by those who believe and know the truth" (4:4, NAB). When I went to say goodbye to an elderly cancer patient and his wife, happy to see them leave the hospital, we prayed, joining hands and thanking God for having brought us together and for taking care of him all those days.

4. The prayer of acceptance and thanks for God's will

Another occasion for evangelizing and familiarizing our brothers and sisters with God's word is when we try to make them aware of how God's will works in our lives and how we must always want to do his will, not ours, even in the face of suffering. Sometimes what the patients need to accept is not their present illness but some circumstance in their lives that is making them miserable and despondent. A woman told me of her unhappiness at having to move to a small and rather dull town because her husband had bought a house there. "Diana," I said to her, "God is in control of our lives, particularly if we allow him *to be God* and believe in him and accept the things he allows, because he loves you. You know, we also have a place I complain about every time I forget that God allowed us to acquire it when we did. Look what God says about accepting his will for us." And I read to her Ephesians 5:17, 20:

> Therefore, do not continue in ignorance, but try to understand what is the will of the Lord...giving thanks always and

97

for everything in the name of our Lord Jesus Christ to God
the Father (NAB).

Bishop Fulton Sheen writes: "Things happen against your will,
but nothing, except sin, happens against God's will,"[69] and quotes
Job's well-known reaction at learning of one of his misfortunes,
"The Lord gave and the Lord has taken away; blessed be the name
of the Lord" (Jb 1:21, NAB). Then he elaborates on this idea and
says what I said to Diana, "All things work for good for those who
love God" (Rom 8:28, NAB), assuring her that "If you trust in God
and surrender to his will, you are always happy."

Many other times it is the suffering from actual illness (and the
depression it may cause when we are spiritually unprepared to
cope) that keeps us from accepting God's will. St. Teresa of Ávila
refers to one of the many times she was feeling miserable at seeing
herself so full of pain and so weary at bedtime: "The Lord appeared
to me and consoled me much, and told me to do [thus, accepting
his will] these things out of love for him...that it was now necessary
for my life." Having experienced that, she would sometimes pray,
"Lord, to die or to suffer; I do not ask you anything else for me."
She adds, "It consoles me to hear the clock, for it seems that I
come nearer to seeing God, as I see that hour of life pass."[70]

Let us remind the sick of how Jesus, knowing he was going to
die on the cross for us, prayed: "Father, if you are willing, take this
cup away from me; still, not my will, but yours be done" (Lk 22:42,
NAB), and with the strength given him by the Holy Spirit he
endured the horror of his passion, triumphing over his suffering
and that of the whole world. Thus, when we see those whose faith
is crumbling under the pressure of suffering, let us think of Paul's
words, "Do not throw away your confidence; it will have great rec-
ompense. You need endurance to do the will of God and receive
what he has promised" (Heb 10:35–36, NAB). Let us make it a
point to add:

Lord, give us the faith and the trust in your love and mercy to thank you for everything you allow to happen in our lives, to offer you these trials, and to remember your words, "My thoughts are not your thoughts, nor are your ways my ways" [Is 55:8, NAB], always keeping in mind that "all things work for good for those who love God" [Rom 8:28, NAB].

5. The prayer of trust, surrender, and hope

Ralph Martin says, "When hardship comes into our lives, the best thing we can do is turn ourselves in and surrender to God. It is less painful in the long run to cooperate with God than to resist him."[71] To do that, we need to learn to trust more in God's unfailing faithfulness and love, particularly when we are in the hospital and our spiritual defenses are lower because of unsettling anxiety, fear, and uncertainty. It is a critical time when patients' very anxiety may often prompt them, although they may be churchgoers, to decline any assistance because they think they would rather be alone. Their words always reflect their state of mind, and we should try to ease their anxiety by assuring them that God is in control of that situation and that they must trust in him. My prayer may be this:

Father, creator of heaven and earth, we praise you and thank you for gathering us together in the name of your Son Jesus, whom you allowed to die on the cross for _____ and for each one of us, that we might be able to come before you as we do right now. Jesus, you said, "when two or more are gathered together in my name, I am in their midst," so we thank you for your presence. We thank you because we know you are compassionate, as your Father is compassionate. Again, Father, we ask you, gathered in this room in the name of your Son Jesus, that you help us to willingly put this situation in your hands and surrender to you, that you grant us the grace of trust and hope. Amen.

God may very well set their hearts at peace through our prayer, better preparing them for whatever may develop. We may even be prompted to add some appropriate Bible verses, such as the well-known, encouraging words in Psalm 23:1-4, or those in Psalm 27: "I believe I shall enjoy the Lord's goodness in the land of the living" (13, NAB), "Wait for the Lord; be of good courage, and he shall strengthen your heart" (14, NKJ), or

> God indeed is my savior; I am confident and unafraid. My strength and my courage is the Lord (Is 12:2, NAB).
>
> I sought the Lord, who answered me, delivered me from all my fears (Ps 34: 4/5, NAB).
>
> When I am afraid, in you I place my trust (Ps 56: 3/4, NAB).

Since we know that "the fear of man brings a snare, but whoever trusts in the Lord will be safe" (Prv 29:25, NAB), I usually ask for protection from any negative thoughts, "as we know they do not come from you, Lord," and try to back my own prayer with God's word, "For whatever things were written before were written for our learning, that we might have hope..." (Rom 15:4, NKJ), very specifically those in Philippians 4:6-7, quoted earlier. We must always remember that when we come before God we should "approach with a sincere heart and in absolute trust" (Heb 10:22, NAB). We may thus contribute to the promised process of holiness,

> knowing that suffering produces endurance, and endurance produces character, and character produces hope, and hope does not disappoint us, because the love of God has been poured into our hearts through the Holy Spirit who has been given to us (Rom 5:3-5).

This is a good occasion for sharing some testimonies, as when I tell them of the time my wife had a major operation to have a small tumor removed from her lung, and how after the first shock, she put her situation in the Lord's hands and was almost never attacked by fear, even before she knew that it was not malignant. In 1996, we were blessed to meet Glen and Emily Ager, of Wycliff Bible Translators. When Glen had to receive treatment for cancer later that year, Emily wrote:

> We're doing quite well, feeling garrisoned and undergirded in prayer. That's the only way we can explain our lack of fear, our confidence in God whatever the future holds, and much peace....We've had tons of encouragement and strength from the family of God and feel satisfied and at peace with what's happening. God is here, blessing and strengthening us.

Describing the fearful and risky radiation treatment, she wrote:

> In many ways, this brush with cancer has been a very rich experience. Rich? Yes, rich. We have seen our tendency to control, which means we don't let God control. We have seen our own anger when things don't go our way. We have seen our terrible helplessness and our desire to manipulate God....

Finally, in March, Glen wrote about the "lessons" he had learned through this experience concerning his spiritual short-comings, asking us to join them in thanking God for having shown him his love in so many ways and "for the *gift* of cancer, for his patient *grace* with me." He closed with these two quotations:

> God disciplines us for our good, that we may share in his holiness. No discipline seems pleasant at the time, but painful. Later on, however, it produces a harvest of right-eousness and peace for those who have been trained by it (Heb 12:10–11)....Now he...will enlarge the harvest of your righteousness. You will be made rich in every way so that you can be generous on every occasion...and your generosity will result in thanksgiving to God (2 Cor 9:10).

Once more we were witnessing the effect of prayer and the presence of that peace that "surpasses all understanding" (Phil 4:7, NAB). As Kenneth Pike, co-founder of Wycliff Bible Translators, writes, clearly thinking of Paul's hopeful words in Romans 5,

> Without hope a person can trust and still be glum.... Hope looks to the hills—to the harvest. "When the plowman plows and the thresher threshes, they ought to do so in hope..." (1 Cor 9:10)...There must be growth. The start is likely to be with faith, in trial.[72]

Thus, hope makes us look ahead without stopping to dwell on present or past situations, fixing our eyes on Jesus, our way, our hope, our light, now and for eternity, if we allow him to draw us into his kingdom. For life is short; it truly is "like a passing shadow" (Ps 144:4, NAB), "like a vapor that appears for a little time and then vanishes away" (Jas 4:14, NKJ). Yet we need to reach that stage in our spiritual journey when we will say, "You are my only hope" (Ps 39:6/7, NAB). We can always be through his word, and witnesses like the Glen and Emily Ager, "strongly encouraged to hold fast to the hope that lies before us" (Heb 6:18, NAB), "as we await the blessed hope" (Ti 2:13, NAB), "Christ Jesus our hope" (1 Ti 1:1, NAB), "a living hope" (1 Pt 1:3, NAB). "Everyone who has this hope in him purifies himself, just as he is pure" (1 Jn 3:3, NAB). I carry in my Bible these prayerful words of hope by Mother Teresa:

> One thing Jesus asks of me: That I lean on him and only in him I put complete trust; that I surrender myself to him unreservedly. Even when all goes wrong and I feel as if I am a ship without a compass, I must give myself completely to him. I must not attempt to control God's action.[73]

The same attitude is found in the closing prayer of the Chaplet of Divine Mercy of Blessed Faustina Kowalska:

Eternal God, in whom mercy is endless and treasure of compassion inexhaustible, look kindly upon us and increase
your mercy in us, that in difficult moments we might not
despair nor become despondent, but with great confidence
submit ourselves to your holy will, which is love and mercy
itself.[74]

6. The prayer offering our suffering

After considering what we learned about suffering in Chapters
1 and 6 and the attitude toward it that God expects from us with
the strength of his Holy Spirit, we realize that there are three
aspects of it that we need to bring to the attention of the sick.
One is that whenever our faith is threatened in suffering we must
immediately cry out to the Lord: "Be my rock and refuge" (Ps
71:3, NAB), or "Lord Jesus, have mercy!" until his peace fills us
and we can once again say, "I kept faith, even when I said, 'I am
greatly afflicted!'" (Ps 116:10, NAB).

The second aspect is the personal use of their own suffering as
an offering to God through Jesus Christ for his own purposes. The
third is offering it for others as a form of intercession. A few years
ago, I read in a British Catholic newspaper John Paul II's message
for the Third World Day of the Sick, where he said:

Called to union with Christ, the Christian, with the acceptance and the offering of suffering, announces the construc-
tive power of the cross...asking him for the strength to
transform the trial afflicting you into a gift.

In his encyclical *Vita Consecrata*, the pope wrote as a mandate
that those who, like us, minister to the sick,

should encourage the sick themselves to offer their sufferings in communion with Christ, crucified and glorified for
the salvation of all and, indeed, they should strengthen in
the sick the awareness of being able to carry out a pastoral

ministry of their own through the specific charism of the cross" (#83).

I was happy to read those words, for I had developed the habit of suggesting to my patients that they lay their suffering at the foot of Jesus' cross, that he may join it to his own suffering for humanity and for the salvation of souls. As John Paul II explains, "It is suffering, more than anything else, which clears the way for the grace which transforms human souls."[75] My prayer may go like this:

> Father, we praise you and thank you for your love; we thank you for giving us your Son Jesus on the cross. O Holy Spirit, fill our mind and heart with the confidence that Jesus is constantly with us, that he never abandons us. And Father, give us the faith and the will to offer you whatever suffering we may go through for the suffering of your Son for us. Be always with _____ , Jesus; fill this room with your presence and that of your angels. Fill_____'s body, heart, and mind with your peace. We thank you and praise you, Jesus. Praise you, Lord, praise you.

I suggest to some patients who are really open to prayer that they offer their suffering for those who do not pray, so that they may say, like St. Paul, "Now I rejoice in my sufferings for your sake" (Col 1:24, NAB). Let us instill in our sick brothers and sisters the assurance that, as Paul tells us, "we are children of God...and joint heirs with Christ, if only we suffer with him so that we may also be glorified with him" (Rom 8:16–17, NAB). Let us share with them God's words on suffering to make their faith grow to that point where they will recognize that they are

> afflicted in every way...but not driven to despair...struck down, but not destroyed [crushed, NKJ]; always carrying about in the body the dying of Jesus, so that the life of Jesus

may also be manifested in our body...in our mortal flesh (2 Cor 4:8–11, NAB).

Inspired by God's word and strengthened by Jesus' body in communion, suffering patients may even appropriate Paul's words, "In my flesh I am filling up what is lacking in the afflictions of Christ for the sake of his body, that is, the Church" (Col 1:24, NAB). Rev. Kossicki confirms this:

All of us can offer our sufferings with Christ, no matter how small they are, no matter what type they are, whether they are physical, emotional, or spiritual. Suffering, offered in union with Christ, is very precious to the Lord. Don't waste it. Offer it up with Christ for the salvation of souls.[76]

Let us ask God that his Holy Spirit will instill in their minds and hearts what Paul said to the Christians of Rome, "I urge you, therefore, brothers, by the mercies of God, to offer your bodies as a living sacrifice" (Rom 12:1, NAB). What better time to do that than when they receive communion, since at that moment Christ is in their own bodies and they are one with Jesus? Donna told me that she offered her suffering for the suffering children, and I could imagine how God would accept that intercession when I prayed with her while she suffered from excruciating pain.

7. The prayer for sadness, anxiety, fear, and despondency

The sixteenth-century Spanish saint, Ignatius of Loyola, assures us in his famous *Spiritual Exercises* that when we desire to grow spiritually "it is characteristic of the evil spirit to harass with anxiety, to afflict with sadness, to raise obstacles backed by fallacious reasoning that disturbs the soul."[77] We are much more vulnerable to this attack when we have been physically, mentally, and spiritually weakened by illness. But if we trust in God's promises and, like the psalm, cry out to him in our hearts, "You are my rock and my fortress" (Ps 31:3/4, NAB), we will also experience the certitude that he cannot abandon us.

> For I am convinced that neither death, nor life, nor angels, nor principalities, nor present things, nor future things, nor powers, nor height, nor depth, nor any other creature will be able to separate us from the love of God in Christ Jesus our Lord (Rom 8:38, NAB).

We must have no doubt that, as Dr. Reed says, "Fear, whether of death or illness, is a tool of Satan used to defeat Christians and to bring all manner of illness and emotional problems." He is "convinced that fear and apprehension cause pain to increase."[78] Therefore, this is the time to advise our brothers and sisters: "Cast all your anxieties on him, for he cares about you" (1 Pet 5:7, RSV), "For you did not receive a spirit of slavery to fall back into fear, but you received a spirit of adoption, through which we cry, "Abba, Father!" (Rom 8:15, NAB), "God has not given us a spirit of fear, but of power and of love and of a sound mind" (2 Tm 1:7, NKJ). Certainly Paul's words in Philippians 4:6–7 cannot be more fitting, which sometimes I explain as I quote or read:

> Have no anxiety about anything, but in everything *[that is, even in this situation, because God does not always want us to understand, but to accept, and this we can achieve by keeping close to him and trusting in him]* by prayer and supplication, with thanksgiving *[for anything God allows to happen in our lives and for his many blessings]*, let your request be made known to God *[so, do it, because he wants us to ask him]*. And the peace of God, which surpasses all understanding *[and which is already healing]*, will keep your hearts and your minds *[so that the devil cannot attack you there]* in Christ Jesus.

It is important that those who are fearful know those promises. Knowing that God's words accomplish the purpose for which they were sent (Is 55:11), let us believe that they will do for their minds and spirits what a pain killer does for their bodies. Besides thanking God for those things that are obviously good, we should endeavor to imprint in their minds how God wants us to thank him in every situation and to trust in him always: "In everything give thanks, for that is the will of God in Christ Jesus for you" (2 Thes 1:18, NKJ). This would not be possible without acceptance—different from passive resignation—since acceptance and trust in God go hand-in-hand. I do not mention faith to them, lest it would sound as if they did not "deserve" to be well for lack of it. A good reading from Jesus' own lips is in John 14:1: "Do not let your hearts be troubled. You have faith in God; have faith also in me" (NAB). If it is a terminal patient, conscious of his or her situation but fearful of death, God may bless that person with his peace as we read these words: "I will come back again and take you to myself, so that where I am you also may be" (Jn 14:3, NAB). Often I suggest that, when they feel the approach of anxiety, fear, or depression, they immediately pray the Jesus prayer, "Lord Jesus Christ, Son of [the living] God, have mercy on me [a sinner]." St. Silouan, the Russian Orthodox mystic who died in 1938, was taught this prayer when he arrived at his monastery in Greece, for it "can be said everywhere and at all times."[79] Since I visited that and other monasteries in Mount Athos, I became very fond of that prayer, a perfect formula to "pray without ceasing" (1 Thes 5:17, NAB).

8. The prayer of forgiveness

Having discussed the problem of unforgiveness in Chapter 7, we can see now how we have to approach and lead in prayer the unforgiving person. We are asking for the grace to forgive, something humanly impossible that God has to put in our hearts, as he puts the grace of love, for forgiveness is but one aspect of love. If we truly forgive, we love the person who hurt us, but if we think that we have "just forgotten," then we have not. We should always, lovingly, and without "preaching" make the unforgiving person aware of the words Jesus gave us when he taught us to pray: "Forgive us our debts as we forgive our debtors" (Mt 6:12, NAB), and of the fact that he adds: "If you do not forgive others, neither will your Father forgive your transgressions" (Mt 6:15, NAB). Often, as I pray the Our Father with a patient, I purposely emphasize the words about forgiveness to bring to their attention a possible need to forgive someone, not only because it is God's command, but because it can bring about healing of physical or emotional problems, so often aggravated by unforgiveness.

> Lord God, creator of heaven and earth, we praise you and glorify you because we can come before you as your children. You, who always love and forgive, ask us to forgive those who have hurt us. But you know how hard it is, you know how_____ has been carrying deep wounds inflicted by others [or here we mention the person who caused them]. Father, you love us so much that you gave your Son Jesus that we might never die but have eternal life. But we know that living with a wounded heart and nurturing unforgiveness is not really living, and that eternal life with you begins here on earth. So, Father, let the blood of your Son Jesus cleanse_____ from his/her unforgiveness and fill his/hear heart with forgiveness, so that he/she may forgive as you forgive. Thank you, Father, thank you, Jesus, thank you, Holy Spirit, for filling our hearts and minds with the desire to forgive.

9. The prayer of intercession: Patients and others

In the Old Testament God already expresses his desire that we pray for others when, for instance, he laments finding no intercessors for his people (Is 59:16; Ez 22:30). With the new covenant he made us all "a royal priesthood" (1 Pet 2:9, NAB) and, as priests, intercessors with our "merciful and faithful high priest" and intercessor, Jesus (Heb 2:18, NKJ), who intercedes for all of us. Rev. Kossicki remarks:

> As members of the Body of Christ, we all have an obligation to pray for one another in the same way Paul did. No one is excused from this obligation...all are called to intercede with Christ.[80]

By this we should understand that, besides praying for those we know and love and for those who request our prayers, there are other subjects for our prayer that fall within that daily obligation: our Church and the unity of the Christian Churches, our parish priests, all priests and pastors in the Christian Churches, all bishops and the pope, the Jewish people, war-torn countries, refugees and those who help them, for protection against terrorism, the unemployed, all the sick in our hospitals, all mothers contemplating abortion and those who perform them, those who are traveling, working in dangerous conditions, and the victims of disasters. In addition, we should learn to back our intercessory prayer with fasting as many Christians do—a unique way to join our brothers and sisters in other Churches—a totally biblical and Christian practice, neglected by many.

Knowing, therefore, the importance of intercession, it should follow that another way we must consider the suffering of those we visit is, as mentioned earlier, as a sacrifice of intercession for others. Sometimes the patient with whom we have engaged in conversation begins to tell us about family problems, for instance, a bad relationship, a relative's sinful habit, or someone else's illness or misfortune that is clearly bothering the patient. In those cases, we cannot remain indifferent. We may offer words of counsel, but anything else, except listening attentively (though not to details we would rather not know, or to gossip), can be superfluous and time-consuming. The best thing is to say, "Well, let's pray about that," and then just lift up that person or situation to God.

Sometimes the patient asks us to pray for others. A woman whose husband made fun of her for going to church, asked me to pray for him, and I did. I encouraged her to offer her suffering for him, which she did. A mother in pediatrics, when I offered to pray for her child, asked me to pray for her little nephew who was undergoing a bone marrow transplant for leukemia. Since she was suffering because her own daughter was suffering, she could certainly be an excellent intercessor precisely at that time.

What is the best way to begin intercession? With praise, by all means. If Jesus himself tells us, "Your Father knows what you need before you ask him" (Mt 6:8, RSV), the emphasis does not have to be in "informing" God of the person's problem with all sorts of details, but in praise. As for everything else, we find beautiful examples of intercessory prayer in the Bible, for instance, in 2 Samuel 7:22-29 and in 2 Kings 19:15-19. Sometimes the prayer begins by a confession and by asking forgiveness, as in Daniel 9:3-5, 9, 17, an important aspect to remember when praying with certain persons. We must note that in these prayers it is only after praise, confession, and repentance, in that order, that they say, "And now, Lord..." (very much like saying, "Now, not before, I am in a position to intercede"), and then the object of their intercession is expressed. Finally, all Christians should appeal to our best intercessor after Jesus, his own Mother, who suffered for him and continues to suffer for the world in her desire to bring us closer to her Son through obedience to him, as she already told us at Cana: "'Do whatever he tells you" (Jn 2:5, NAB).

10. Being prayerfully mindful of the liturgical year

Because patients cannot attend church and sometimes even lose track of feasts and celebrations, it is good to bring those special occasions to their attention when conversing and in our prayer, for instance, during Christmas, Lent and Holy Week, Pentecost, the Ascension and, for Catholics, the Body and Blood of Christ, the Sacred Heart of Jesus, Our Lady of Sorrows, Christ the King, or a particular saint. The Christmas season, specifically Christmas Eve and Christmas Day, is always a special opportunity to refer to the beautiful mystery of Jesus' birth, the long-awaited and announced messiah, our personal savior, and bring to their minds and hearts the reality of the Trinity:

> We thank you, Father for giving us your Son, Jesus, for having given yourself to us in him, and for your infinite love. We thank you, Mary, mother of God the Son and our mother, for bringing Jesus into the world through your own faithfulness and obedience to God the Father and through the action of the Holy Spirit. And we thank you, Jesus, our savior; we thank you because, as we celebrate your birth, we already know that you came to this world to later die on the cross for each one of us that we may be forgiven and be with you for eternity.

There are always those who must spend Christmas Day in the hospital. The Christmas trees and decorations with which the hospital staff on each unit tries to create a homey atmosphere are certainly appreciated by the patients but cannot replace their being home with their families. I enjoy making Christmas cards and giving the patients individually addressed, handwritten copies on behalf of "The R.C. Pastoral Care Team." One year the message was: "Dear_____: 'He will be with you and will never fail you or forsake you. So do not fear or be dismayed' (Deuteronomy 31:8). Therefore, whether we are at home or in the hospital, we can celebrate Jesus' birthday, for we know that he came to die for each of us that we might be with him always." They truly appreciate it. When I pray with them at that time, I also like to seek the intercession of Jesus' parents, Mary and Joseph, of the whole Holy Family, asking them:

Please, Mary and Joseph, allow_____to hold your baby
Jesus in his/her arms, that he may touch him/her and make
him/her well as a gift of his mercy, for you brought him into
the world, Mary, through the Father's love, for our salvation.

I also enjoy praying with patients on New Year's Day, when we
can join them in thanking the Lord for the past year and asking
his blessing for the new one.

We thank you, Lord, for everything you have given us in the
past year and for everything you have allowed to happen in
our lives. We offer you, Lord, any suffering we may have
gone through to join the suffering of your Son Jesus for us.
We ask you to bless our brother/sister in the New Year, to
give him/her your peace and keep him/her always mindful
of your love and faithfulness.

Then, when Lent comes and all Christian Churches draw closer
to our celebration of our Lord's passion, death, and resurrection,
especially during Holy Week, I find it a very special time, as I talk
to them or pray, to refer to the full, awesome meaning of the sacrament of the Eucharist: "What a great privilege it is to bring you
the body of Jesus, now that we are celebrating his death on the
cross for you, for me, for each one of us." At that time I also give
them a card, saying, for instance: "Dear_____: Jesus died for all,
that those who live should live no longer for themselves, but for
him who died and rose again." And on Easter Sunday and the
days that follow, I include in my prayer with them something like
this:

We thank you, Father, for giving us your Son Jesus on the
cross; we thank you, Jesus, for dying for us on that cross,
because thanks to that we are now receiving your body.
Thank you, Jesus. We praise you and glorify you for leaving
us this wonderful gift through our Church.

Occasionally with my Catholic patients, I like to share one of the readings of the day's mass, so often words of hope and trust in God, on his faithfulness and love. Recently, for instance, the day's gospel reading was Jesus' healing of Bartimaeus's blindness (Mk 10: 48–52), after which he follows Jesus; the other was from Jeremiah 31:8, about God bringing back from exile ("our separation from him") "the blind and the lame" (NAB). Although I was not scheduled for the hospital that Sunday, I went to see a man for whom I had prayed the day before, whose vision had deteriorated. I took him and his wife to a Quiet Room, where briefly but prayerfully I shared those two readings with them and prayed a short prayer of praise and intercession, asking Jesus to touch him for his glory as he touched Bartimaeus and bring him closer to him. I thought afterward, "How could I bring Jesus to him if I didn't bring also, in my mind or actually in my hands, Jesus' word?" A few days later someone told me he had said that his vision had improved very much after that prayer.

Another time I had to visit two men in ICU. One seemed unconscious, but I always remember now Dr. William Reed's words concerning the unconscious patient, that "anyone who is asleep or comatose should be treated as if he were awake and able to comprehend," and how he recommends prayer and "positive suggestions relative to the patient's recovery and his state in general."[81] So I held his hand, greeted him, and told him I wished to read to him something from the psalm of the day: "Lord, hear my prayer, listen to my cry for help. In this time of trouble I call, for you will answer me" (Ps 86:6–7, NAB). I then continued with a short prayer asking Jesus to fill his body, heart, and mind with his healing peace. Many psalms express trust in the Lord, such as psalms 23, 27:13, and Isaiah 26:1–6, and if we make the day's readings part of our own morning prayer, we will most of the time find opportunities to either refer to them or actually read them from the Bible.

11. Ecumenism in the hospital: Promoting the unity of the Body of Christ

Last Christmas, while trying to find a refrigerator for a man who could not afford one, I called the Fredericton Food Bank. A woman answered the phone who remembered me: "My name is Sharon. You probably don't remember me, but you prayed for me when you came to visit my roommate. I am a Seventh Day Adventist. When you left I thought, 'That's being a Christian!'"

As a Catholic pastoral care visitor, I do not go around offering to pray for the non-Catholic patients I meet, since I know they have their own clergy and lay ministers. By now, however, I must have prayed with those from every Christian denomination. I cannot just ignore, particularly in a double room, the other brother or sister, especially when I see they need prayer. By doing this, let us not forget, we are healing our separation a little bit. A prophecy at a 1977 ecumenical conference of 40,000 people in Kansas City said: "The Body of my Son is broken," after which all those brothers and sisters fell to their knees and wept, as God's people did in repentance in Ezra 10:1.[82]

A nurse once led me to a young man who said he needed to talk to me. I went and sat on his bed. He had diabetes, poor eyesight, and painful hands and wrists from arthritis. He could not play his guitar, but he let me read one of his own songs about his rough life and "the world's lack of compassion and charity." He said he worshiped in different churches and prayed daily and that thanks to prayer he had been able to abandon heavy drinking and drugs. I laid a hand on his hands and prayed. The next day he was with a Pentecostal friend. I said that three gathered together in his name was even better, and I led them in prayer.

One day as I offered prayer for a Catholic patient, his roommate asked me whether I could pray for him too. When I learned he was Anglican, I said how wonderful it would be for us to pray together. An Anglican woman who heard me came in. I invited her to join

114

us, closed the door "for our little ecumenical service," I said, prayed for us all, and then we ended with the Our Father, after which I gave communion to my patient. They loved it.

Usually, if only out of courtesy, we have to talk to the other patient, in which case I may ask them if their pastoral care visitors have come. Then I explain that I can pray for both and give communion to my Catholic patient; they invariably accept the idea most gladly. A woman from the Salvation Army said afterward, "I'll never forget it." Another time I had to explain briefly to a Baptist that we Catholics pray to Mary as our intercessor, but we do not "worship" her, as some think out of innocent ignorance, only "venerate" her as the mother of God the Son. To a United Church woman I explained where most of the words of the Hail Mary come from (Lk 1:28, 42); another told me she prayed to Jesus and Mary nightly.

I hasten to say that I never do this indiscriminately, but when I do, it is a beautiful occasion to be united with non-Catholic Christians, dispel misconceptions, and draw brothers or sisters in Christ closer to each other. The reaction is always extremely positive. I wish ministers or lay pastoral caregivers from all Churches felt the freedom in the Spirit to do likewise, since we know that our Lord prayed to the Father, "that they may all be one...that they may be one as we are one" (Jn 17:21–22, NAB).

Led by "mistakes" to someone who truly needed prayer and comfort, I once approached "the wrong" patient in a double room, a Baptist woman. As we began to talk, I realized it was no mistake, for she was in great need of prayer and was very grateful. Another time I went to the "wrong room" only to find a Spirit-filled Pentecostal woman whom I knew but had not seen in years. She had just lost a leg to cancer, but she radiated joy and peace and we worshiped and praised God together.

Meeting with a patient's relatives, particularly outside the Intensive Care unit, can also be an occasion for promoting ecumenical understanding. Once I tried to see a young man who had been in a bad car accident, from which his wife and another passenger had come out unscathed. The small lounge next to ICU was packed with relatives, so I greeted them, introduced myself and sat down. I told them that we were praying for him at mass, at home, and in our prayer group, and I prayed for him there. I may even have asked for Mary's intercession, I do not remember. The following morning I returned to see them again, and I learned that, apart from the patient and his wife and parents, all the others were Pentecostals. I told them what a pity it was they did not know some of the books in the Catholic Bible, and read to them what God says about patients, physicians, and himself in Sirach 38. I also told them about today's healing ministry in the Catholic Church and in other Churches, about how the great Pentecostal David DuPlessis was invited to speak on the Holy Spirit at Vatican Council II in Rome, how some Pentecostals and Anglicans such as Agnes Sanford had been an influence in the Catholic spiritual renewal in the mid-1960s, and how much I had enjoyed being associated with the Episcopalian Dr. Reed and his interdenominational CMF. They were thrilled, and those Catholics and Pentecostals became, I felt, a little closer to each other.

Naturally, we must be well informed regarding our own Church and our beliefs in general, in case a non-Catholic should comment on issues like those discussed in Appendix III below. But I also enjoy sharing with non-Catholics stories of extraordinary witnesses in their own Churches, such as the Lutheran Dietrich Bonhoeffer (a victim of the Nazis, like St. Maximilian Kolbe), the Episcopalians Dennis and Rita Bennett (Dr. Reed's sister), and others. I particularly enjoy talking about the dedicated pastors or lay persons I have met myself, through whom the Holy Spirit has worked so many signs and wonders.

When I ponder the holiness found in every Christian Church, how Jesus, who died for his Church, wants us united, and how every time we come together we are witnessing and, in different ways, evangelizing, I remember the Trappistine Sr. Maria Gabriela of the Unity (beatified by John Paul II in 1983), who in 1936 offered her life for the unity of all Christians and died three years later. John Paul II exhorts us to repentance and conversion and to prayer for Christian unity, since "In the deep personal dialogue which each of us must carry on with the Lord in prayer, concern for unity cannot be excluded." In a place like a hospital, our interaction and prayer with members of different Churches will confirm that "in the eyes of the world, cooperation among Christians becomes a form of common Christian witness and a means of evangelization which benefits all involved."[83]

Appendix I:
Dealing with Difficult Catholics

"I think priests should marry" is a typical statement among some Catholics today. If we pastoral caregivers love our Church and adhere to her teaching until she tells us otherwise, we can explain that the Church, with very specific exceptions (when a married Anglican priest is ordained a Catholic priest), chooses those who are and intend to remain celibate. Jesus, a celibate himself, tells us that "Not all can accept this word [not to marry], but only those to whom that is granted...because they have renounced marriage for the sake of the kingdom of heaven" (Mt 19:11,12, NAB). St. Paul explains that if a "married man is anxious about the things of the world...he is divided," unable to concentrate on "the things of the Lord" (1 Cor 7:32, 33, NAB)." He advocates celibacy "for the sake of propriety and adherence to the Lord without distraction" (1 Cor 7:35, NAB). Thus, the Church speaks of those called to "consecrate themselves with undivided heart to the Lord" and adds that "accepted with a joyous heart celibacy radiantly proclaims the Reign of God" (*CCC*, #1579). In fact, it should be "a sign of witness to the world...renouncing some undeniable good things...and the good of married life."[84] Although the Eastern Churches allow priests (not bishops) to be married before

ordination, not after, "priestly celibacy is held in great honor... [and many] have freely chosen celibacy for the sake of the Kingdom of God" (*CCC,* #1580). The Roman Catholic Church made celibacy a rule only in the thirteenth century, after priests and religious men and women had chosen that state since the beginning of the Christian Church.

"Women should be ordained priests" is another remark we come across. As with other "controversial" issues, we might remind them that Jesus was the model for the Christian priesthood, just as Aaron and his male descendants were for the Jewish people when God anointed them to offer sacrifices on the altar (Ex 28:1). But Jesus did not offer a sacrifice on any altar; he offered himself as a living sacrifice and thus "the source of eternal salvation...declared by God high priest" (Heb 5:9-10, NAB). Then, after his resurrection,

> Jesus set apart the apostles to lead the early church....The apostles laid hands on the elders they selected to continue their ministry, and so the sacrament of "holy order" or ordination was begun....The fact is that in spite of the evident respect that Jesus had for women, he did not select a woman to be among his twelve apostles. The early church followed his practice...no women priests are mentioned, even in the later periods of the church's early development.[85]

As with celibacy, only if God inspired the pope and his bishops to accept women into the priesthood would the Church overturn this twenty-centuries-old practice.

The conservative or pre-Vatican II Catholic. Some Catholics who lived as adults before the Vatican II Council tell us that the *mass should be in Latin.* I explain that when the first Christians spoke Greek, both the Bible and mass had to be in Greek for many years; that later, Latin began to replace Greek as the language of the people and the Bible had to be translated into Latin (as St.

Jerome did) and mass celebrated in Latin; that when new languages developed and the Bible began to be translated into those languages (John Wycliff in English, Martin Luther in German), the mass continued to be said in Latin for centuries well beyond the time when it no longer responded to the reality of people's languages; and that Vatican II in the mid-1960s decreed that each people should follow the mass in their own language so that both adults and children alike might fully participate in it.

Another thing those people may reject is giving their fellow parishioners *the peace of Christ* at mass. The members of a beautiful three-generation extended family in my parish take communion directly in the mouth and on their knees, the women and the little girls wear veils, and at least the women remain on their knees with their eyes closed while we share the peace of Christ. I admire their devotion, but always wondered about their rejection of such a basic external token of mutual acknowledgment within the body of Christ. I have had many occasions to enjoy cross-cultural differences in this respect; for instance, in Japan we bow to each other, in India we join palms perpendicular to the chest in the "namaste" greeting, in the Maronite rite one person offers the right hand and the other encloses it with the two hands and then slides them back.

Lay Eucharistic ministers is also something many pre-Vatican II Catholics reject.[86] Once a woman I knew from church told me she would not take communion from a lay person. I did not explain that in 1973 Pope Paul VI authorized men and women as Eucharistic ministers. However, I agreed with their complaint about their parish not having *kneelers in the pews* and others having removed them—thus being kept from kneeling—and thought of Paul quoting Isaiah 45:23, "As I live, said the Lord, every knee shall bend before me" (Rom 14:11, NAB), and saying in Philippians 2:10 that "at the name of Jesus every knee should bend, on those in heaven and on earth and under the earth" (NAB).[87]

Appendix II:
The Catholic Church
on Intercommunion

An Anglican priest once told me in the hospital that he sometimes prayed with Roman Catholic patients and even offered them communion. However in *The Documents of Vatican II* we read:

> The ecclesial Communities separated from us...especially because of the lack of the sacrament of Holy Orders...have not preserved the genuine and total reality of the Eucharistic mystery. Nevertheless, when they commemorate the Lord's death and resurrection in the Holy Supper, they profess that it signifies life in communion with Christ and wait his coming in glory.[88]

And the *Catechism of the Catholic Church* specifies that

> When, in the Ordinary's judgment, a grave necessity arises, Catholic ministers may give the sacraments of Eucharist, penance, and anointing of the sick to other Christians...who ask for them of their own will, provided they give evidence of holding the Catholic faith regarding these sacraments and possess the required dispositions (#1401).

Catholics believe that "Because there is one bread, we who are many are one body, for we all partake of the one bread" (1 Cor 10:16-17, RSV) and thus cannot separate sharing that "one bread" and belonging to the same "one body." But we Christians are not one body yet, and one of the most important points of dissension is precisely whether the bread and wine Jesus offered when instituting the Eucharist at the Last Supper (Jn 6:55-56; 1 Cor 11:23-25) becomes his true body and blood at consecration. Most Anglicans regard what they receive in communion only as a symbol, while others share the Catholic belief in Eucharistic transubstantiation; Lutherans believe in consubstantiation (the body and blood of Christ remaining afterward only as wafer and wine). Thus, as Alan Schreck explains;

> Catholics cannot in good conscience participate in communion services in other Christian churches, nor allow other Christians to receive the Eucharist in the Catholic Church...For Catholics, the reception of the Eucharist also expresses their communion or unity with the whole Catholic Church and its elders [while we still witness the present] pain of the divisions that prevent Catholics from sharing the Lord's Supper with other Christians.[89]

Appendix III:
Catholic Issues
for Non-Catholics

One of the points we sometimes need to explain to non-Catholics is that *Catholics pray* to *Mary* because they venerate, not worship, her as Jesus' mother, and that the ancient Hail Mary mostly repeats the words found in Luke 1:28, 42, first by the Angel Gabriel when he appeared to Mary, then by her cousin Elizabeth as she welcomes her.

On the deeply-set issue of *worshiping idols* in our images, one must assure them that none of the biblical references to the images and idols condemned by God, as in Isaiah 42:17, could ever apply to Catholic images of Jesus, Mary, and the saints. Christ on the cross is a reminder of his sacrifice for our salvation; through her images, Mary is remembered as Jesus' mother and our intercessor; and those of saints represent holy men and women held as models of faith and obedience to God, whom we revere as intercessors. Chapters 44 through 49 of the book of Sirach are an account of great biblical men that begins: "Now will I praise those godly men" (NAB). St. Teresa of Ávila writes of when she was led to a deeper conversion in the presence of a crucifix:

> I saw an image...of Christ, with many wounds, and...when I looked at it I was much disturbed to see him like that, for it

represented what he went through for us....I fell prostrated at his feet with much tear-shedding, entreating him to strengthen me so that I would not offend him any more....I profited from it, for I improved since then.[90]

When we are asked about *those books in the Catholic Bible* (the seven deuterocanonical books), we can explain that about A.D. 200, Christians and Jews fixed a definitive list of the sacred books—although the Jews of Palestine took out the seven added by the Greek-speaking Jews—kept in the Christian Bible when in the fourth century it was translated from Greek into Latin. Then, after more than 1500 years of Christianity, Protestants removed them, believing that the original Christian Old Testament had not included them, since the Christians at that time took as a model the one used by the Jews of their own days. Today Catholics and Protestants together are publishing some complete editions of the Bible and many Protestants are discovering the beauty and spiritual richness of those books.

As for the Catholic belief in Jesus' *real presence in the Blessed Sacrament,* mentioned in Appendix II, we know there is a "burning desire [for the Christian Churches] to join in celebrating the one Eucharist of the Lord, and this desire itself is already a common prayer."[91] Some ask about Catholic adoration of the Blessed Sacrament, which reminds me of a Lutheran pastor who, after admitting he could not understand exposition of the Blessed Sacrament, relates how "the real breakthrough came that night when I experienced my first holy hour [in front of the Blessed Host]. Suddenly, I was without argument, and could only exclaim with St. Thomas, 'My Lord and my God!'"[92]

Regarding *ecumenism,* both Catholic and non-Catholic pastoral care workers can promote unity among Christians. In John Paul II's 1995 encyclical *Ut Unum Sint (That They May Be One)* we read:

If Christians, despite their divisions, can grow ever more united in common prayer around Christ, they will grow in the awareness of how little divides them in comparison to what unites them (#22).

Notes

1. Other references to, and quotations from, other Catholic or non-Catholic spiritual literature, the writings of saints, some of the papal encyclicals, or the new *Catechism of the Catholic Church*, are rigorously based on the word of God.

2. Both quotations in *The Word Among Us* (Oct. 30, 1994). Taken from "Homily on the Gospel of Saint John" (XVII.8) and "On the Grace of Christ" (XXVI.27). For complete texts, see Erich Pryzywara, ed., *An Augustine Synthesis* (New York: Harper, 1958).

3. *Divine Mercy in My Soul: The Diary of Sister M. Faustina Kowalska* (Stockbridge, Mass.: Marian Press, 1987).

4. Among many others, for instance, St. Thérèse of Lisieux (d. 1897) and Padre Pio (d. 1968).

5. Abbreviated hereafter as *CCC*.

6. Literature, conferences, and retreats on this subject are now well known among Catholics and non-Catholics alike. See, for instance, Kenneth McCall, *Healing the Family Tree* (London: Sheldon Press, 1982); John Hampsch, *Healing Our Family Tree* (Huntington, Ind.: Our Sunday Visitor, 1989).

7. One of the so-called deuterocanonical books, included in the Bible until the fifteenth century, later only in Catholic editions and today again in some others as well.

126

8. William S. Reed, *Surgery of the Soul: Healing the Whole Person: Spirit, Mind and Body* (Tampa: Christian Medical Foundation, 1995), pp. 106–07.

9. "Message for the Third World Day of the Sick."

10. Encyclical *Christifidelis Laici*, 1988, #14.

11. *Crossing The Threshold of Hope* (New York/Toronto: Alfred A. Knopf, 1994), pp. 111–12.

12. ECT stands for the statement "Evangelicals and Catholics Together." In C. Colson and J. Neuhaus, eds., *Evangelicals and Catholics Together* (Dallas/London: World Publishing, 1995), pp. xv–xxxiii.

13. Kenneth L. Pike, *With Heart and Mind: A Personal Synthesis of Scholarship and Devotion* (Duncanville, Tex.: Adult Learning Systems, 1996), p. 13.

14. Judith F. van Heukelem, "'Weep With Those who Weep': Understanding and Helping the Crying Person," *Journal of Psychology and Theology*, 7 (no.2) (1979): 83–84.

15. Ibid., p. 86, from J. R. W. Stott, "When should a Christian weep?" *Christianity Today*, 14 (1969): pp. 3–5.

16. Ibid., p. 86.

17. New York: Pillar Books, 1976.

18. William S. Reed, *Surgery of the Soul*, p. 140 (quoting his colleague, the German psychiatrist Karlfried Graf Von Dürkheim).

19. Paul Tournier, *A Doctor's Casebook in the Light of the Bible* (San Francisco: Harper & Row, 1974), p. 180.

20. Francis MacNutt, *The Prayer that Heals* (Notre Dame, Ind.: Ave María Press, 1981), p. 43.

21. Some Bibles count psalm titles or dedications as the first verse. In editions where this occurs, the number after the slash (/) indicates the verse to which we refer.

22. "Dogmatic Constitution on Divine Revelation," Chapter VI, "Sacred Scripture in the Life of the Church" (#25), *The Documents of Vatican II.*

23. Murray, who died in 1918, wrote many books, among them *The Prayer Life* (Springdale, Penn.: Whitaker House, 1981), Chapter 1.

24. Barbara Shlemon, *To Heal as Jesus Healed* (Notre Dame, Ind.: Ave Maria Press, 1978), p. 43.

25. Sharon Fish and Judith Allen Shelly. *Spiritual Care: The Nurse's Role* (Downers Grove, Ill.: InterVarsity Press, 1978), pp. 110, 111.

26. We can read this text, for instance, in John A. Hardon, S.J., *A Treasury of Catholic Wisdom* (New York: Doubleday, 1987), pp. 1–9, a collection of texts by thirty-three of the greatest Christian thinkers and writers from the beginning of Christianity.

27. For Catholics, independently of the Church's few strictly prescribed occasions.

28. *Diary* (#1487).

29. Thomas à Kempis, *The Imitation of Christ.* (Orleans, Mass.: Paraclete Press, 1996), IV, 1.11.

30. My translation from *Vida de Santa Teresa de Jesús escrita por ella misma.* In S. de Santa Teresa, C.D., ed., *Obras de Santa Teresa* (Burgos: El Monte Carmelo, 1922). See J.M. Cohen, trans., *The Life of Saint Teresa by Herself* (Hamondsworth: Penguin, 1957).

31. *Miracles Do Happen* (Ann Arbor, Mich.: Servant Books, 1987), pp. 55–68.

32. *A Treasury of Catholic Wisdom*, p. 218.

33. *Life*, XXXVIII.19.

34. *The Autobiography of Saint Margaret Mary Alacoque* (Rockford, Ill: Tan Books, 1952), #30.

35. *The Imitation of Christ*, IV, 1.12.

36. *Diary*, #1804, #1811.

37. My translation of *Camino de Perfección*. In *Obras de Santa Teresa*, XXXIV.12. See Benedict Zimmerman, ed., *The Way of Perfection* (Rockford, Ill.: Tan Books, 1997).

38. *The Imitation of Christ*, 1V, 12.4.

39. *The Documents of Vatican II, Constitution on the Sacred Liturgy*, Chapter III, "The Other Sacraments and the Sacramentals" (#73).

40. Barbara Shlemon, *Healing Prayer* (Notre Dame, Ind.: Ave Maria Press, 1976), pp. 13-16. Also "The Healing Power of the Eucharist," a leaflet from Our Lady of Divine Providence, 702 Bayview Ave., Clearwater, Florida.

41. Very interesting details concerning the development of the sacrament of reconciliation can be found in the section on confession in Alan Shreck, *Catholic and Christian: An Explanation of Commonly Misunderstood Catholic Beliefs* (Ann Arbor: Servant Books, 1984), pp. 137-40; also in Paul A. Feider, *The Sacraments: Encountering With the Risen Lord* (Notre Dame, Ind.: Ave Maria Press, 1986), Chapter 4. See, in general, the *Catechism of the Catholic Church* (#1440-1470).

42. In his 1984 encyclical *Salvifici Doloris*, #8.

43. *Diary*, #286.

44. *Salvifici Doloris*, #10.

45. Ralph Martin, *Called to Holiness* (Ann Arbor, Mich.: Servant Books, 1988), p. 128.

46. Ralph Martin, "When Trials Weigh You." *New Covenant* (August 1994).

47. *Salvifici Doloris*, #24.

48. Raniero Cantalamesa, O.F.M., "In Love With Eternity." *New Covenant* (Nov. 1992), from his book *Jesus Christ: The Holy One of God* (Collegeville, Minn.: Liturgical Press, 1992).

49. Ralph Martin, *Called to Holiness*, p. 74.

50. Raniero Cantalamessa, O.F.M., *Ungidos por el Espíritu* (Anointed by the Spirit), p. 79 (based on a retreat he gave for Latin American priests and bishops).

51. "Forgiveness: Digging Up the Root of Bitterness." *New Covenant* (September 1991): 7–10.

52. Lance Morrow, "I Spoke...As a Brother." *Time* (January 9, 1984): 28.

53. Corrie ten Boom, *Tramp for the Lord* (New York: Pillar Books, 1976), pp. 53–55.

54. Richard Wurmbrand, *Tortured for Christ* (New York: Bantam Books, 1977), p. 43.

55. *"The Admonitions,"* XXVI. In *A Treasury of Catholic Wisdom*, p. 225.

56. Head of a Christian psychiatry program at Duke University and author of *The Grace to Grow* (Waco, Tex.: Word Books), on healing prayer in his practice.

57. George W. Kossicki, C.S.B., *Intercession: Moving Mountains by*

Living Eucharistically (Milford, Ohio: Faith Publishing Company, 1996), p. 15.

58. *Introduction to the Devout Life, XI.* In *A Treasury of Catholic Wisdom*, p. 534.

59. Ibid., XII, p. 536.

60. Ibid., XI, p. 534.

61. *Surgery of the Soul*, pp. 79–80.

62. Ibid., p. 54.

63. Paul Tournier, *The Seasons of Life* (Atlanta: John Knox Press, 1977), pp. 55, 61.

64. *Surgery of the Soul*, p. 88.

65. *To Heal as Jesus Healed*, p. 43.

66. Francis MacNutt, *Healing* (Notre Dame, Ind.: Ave Maria Press, 1974; New York: Bantam Books, 1977).

67. Agnes Sanford, *The Healing Light* (New York: Ballantine Books, 1983), *Sealed Orders: The Autobiography of a Christian Mystic* (North Brunswick: Bridge-Logos, 1972); A. Sanford, ed., *The Healing Gifts of the Spirit* (Berkhamstead, Hertfordshire: Arthur James, Ltd., 1990).

68. Dietrich Bonhoeffer, *Life Together: The Classical Explanation of Faith in Community* (San Francisco: Harper & Row, 1993), p. 17.

69. Fulton Sheen, *Preface to Religion, "Hope."* In *A Treasury of Catholic Wisdom*, p. 717.

70. *Life*, XI.20.

71. Ralph Martin, "Hardship and Holiness." *New Covenant* (Nov. 1987).

72. Kenneth L. Pike, *With Heart and Mind: A Personal Synthesis of Scholarship and Devotion* (Duncanville, Tex.: Adult Learning Systems, 1996), p. 84.

73. Mother Teresa, *Total Surrender*, Br. Angelo Devananda, ed. (Ann Arbor: Servant Publications, 1989), pp. 39–40.

74. *Diary*, #950,

75. John Paul II, *Salvifici Doloris*, #27.

76. *Intercession*, p. 50.

77. *Spiritual Exercises, "Rules for the Discernment of Spirits."* In *A Treasury of Catholic Wisdom*, p. 408.

78. *Surgery of the Soul*, pp. 79, 152.

79. Archimandrite Sophroni, *The Monk of Mount Athos: Staretz Silouan 1866–1938* (Crestwood, N.Y.: Saint Vladimir's Press, 1973), p. 17. And Archimandrite Sophroni, *Wisdom From Mount Athos: The Writings of Staretz Silouan* 1866-1938 (Crestwood, N.Y.: St. Vladimir's Seminary Press, 1974). See F. Poyatos, "Mount Athos: Soul's Haven on Earth," *Queen's Quarterly*, Vol. 105 (Winter 1997): 660–678.

80. *Intercession*, p. 7.

81. *Surgery of the Soul*, p. 93.

82. Fr. Cantalamessa, who was at that conference (where Ruth Carter was one of the speakers), refers to this prophecy in the above-mentioned book, *Ungidos por el Espíritu.*

83. *Ut Unum Sint*, #27, #40. There are books and documents on ecumenism which pastoral care workers should be conversant with, since they would greatly assist them in understanding the great need for Christian unity, for example "Decree on Ecumenism," in *Documents of Vatican II*, Colson and Neuhaus's *Evangelicals and Catholics Together.*

84. Alan Shreck, *Catholic and Christian* (Ann Arbor, Mich.: Servant Books, 1984), p. 144.

85. Ibid., pp. 144, 147.

86. Stated in "Instruction and Facilitating Communion in Particular Circumstances," published by the Congregation for Divine Worship.

87. Pope John Paul II, echoing the wishes of his predecessor, Paul VI, in a 1980 visit to Germany, said regarding not kneeling, "I am not in favor of it...neither will I recommend it!" (*The Catholic Times*, Vol. 4, No. 2).

88. "Decree on Ecumenism," Chapter III, #22. See also the *Catechism of the Catholic Church*, #1400.

89. *Catholic and Christian*, pp. 135–36.

90. *Life*, IX.1.

91. John Paul II, encyclical, *Ut Unum Sint* (That They May Be One), #45.

92. William J. Cork, B.S.C.D., "A Protestant Looks at the Catholic Charismatic Renewal," *New Covenant* (May 1992): 15–16.

Index of Biblical Quotations

(See note #21, page 128, concerning slash marks within biblical references)

Old Testament

Genesis 1:26; 1:27; 2:7; 3:1, 11
Exodus 28:1
Leviticus 19:18; 20:7
Deuteronomy 6:5; 8:3; 31:8
1 Samuel 1:27–28; 18:10
2 Samuel 1:12; 7:22–29; 12:15, 16; 22:2–3
1 Kings 17:21; 21:22, 27
2 Kings 4:35; 19:15–19; 22:19
Ezra 8:21; 10:1
Esther 4:16
Tobit 12:8
2 Chronicles 20:2–3
2 Maccabees 6:12–13
Job 1:21; 3:1; 5:18; 12:2; 16:2; 38:2–4; 42:5; 42:5–6
Psalms 5:3/4; 6:8; 13:1-2/2-3; 13:5-6/6-7; 16:8-9; 18:2/3; 22:3; 23; 23:1-4; 23:4; 25:7; 27:13-14; 27:14; 31:2-3/3-4; 31:2-3/3-4; 31:3/4; 34:1/2; 34:2/3; 34:4/5; 34:19-20; 34:8/9; 35:13; 35:22; 37:8; 39:6-7; 44:8/9; 50:23; 56:3/4; 57:1/2; 71:8;

72:15; 83:1; 86:1, 7, 17; 86:6-7; 71:3; 88:13; 89:26/27; 103:1-3; 116:10; 139:4; 139:13-16; 143:4, 6, 7; 144:4; 147:1

Proverbs 12:25; 14:13; 14:30; 18:10; 29:25

Ecclesiastes 3:7

Song of Songs 2:9; 2:10

Wisdom 3:1, 5; 3:7; 16:28

Sirach (Ecclesiasticus) 13:24-25; 28:2, 3, 6; 38:1, 9, 12; 30:23; 38:6-7; 44:1

Isaiah 1:18; 8:10; 9:6; 12:2; 26:16; 42:17; 44:22; 45:23; 50:4; 53:5-7; 54:1; 54:4; 55:6; 55:8; 55:11

Jeremiah 1:5; 1:6, 8; 4:14; 16:19; 17:9; 18:6; 28:9; 31:8; 31:13; 32:17

Lamentations 3:23

Ezekiel 2:9; 3:1, 4; 18:21; 18:21-23

Daniel 9:3; 9:3–5, 9,17

Hosea 6:1; 6:6; 5:15

Joel l 2:12

Obadiah 3

Jonah 3:5

Micah 7:18

Zecchariah 1:3

New Testament

Matthew 4:2; 4:4; 4:24; 5:15; 5:16; 5:17; 6:8; 6:12; 6:12-15; 6:15; 7:7; 7:14; 7:29; 9:13; 9:15; 9:20; 10:8; 11:25; 16:18; 16:19; 17:21; 18:8; 18:18; 18:20; 18:21-35; 18:22; 19:11,12; 19:26; 20:1-16; 20:28; 21:22; 22:75; 23:10; 25:36; 25:40; 26:39; 26:26; 26:54; 28:20

Mark 1:27; 1:35; 2:7; 6:7, 13; 9:29; 10:48-52; 12:28-31; 12:34; 16:15; 16:18

Luke 1:28, 42; 1:41; 4:18; 6:9; 6:27-28; 7;15:7; 10:2; 13:2-3; 13:11; 11:10; 15:1; 17:11-19; 17:37-38; 22:42

John 1:4; 1:9; 2:5; 3:16; 4:24; 6:55–56; 8:12; 8:43; 9:2; 11:35; 12:36; 12:46; 14:1; 14:3; 16:13; 17:21-22; 18:37; 20:22-23; 21:16
Acts 1:8; 2:10; 13:2-3; 13:4; 14:23; 15:23; 16:14; 20:35
Romans 5:3; 5:3-5; 5:5; 8:15; 8:16-18; 8:16-17; 8:18; 8:26; 8:27; 8:28; 8:38; 10:17; 12:1; 12:14, 17; 14:11; 15:4; 15:16
1 Corinthians 4:1; 6:19; 7:32, 33; 7:35; 9:10; 9:16; 10:13; 10:10-17; 11:23-25; 11:24; 12:13; 13:1
2 Corinthians 1:3; 1:3-4; 4:8-11; 4:17; 5:20; 6:4-5; 6:20; 9:10; 17:10; 1:27; 12:9
Galatians 2:20; 4:14; 6:2
Ephesians 1:22-23; 5:6; 5:12; 5:20; 5:17, 20; 6:11; 6:12; 6:17
Philippians 2:10; 2:13; 4:6-7; 4:7
Colossians 1:24
1 Thessalonians 4:13-14; 5:17; 5:18; 5:23
2 Thessalonians 1:18
1 Timothy 4:4
2 Timothy 1:7; 3:16-17
Titus 2:13
Hebrews 5:9-10; 2:18; 4:12; 7:25; 10:25; 12:6; 12:10-11; 12:14; 13:8; 13:15; 18:22; 35:36
James 2:8-9; 4:14; 5:10; 5:14-15; 5:16
1 Peter 1:3; 2:9; 3:9; 5:7
1 John 1:9; 3:3; 4:18; 4:20; 5:19
Revelation 3:20; 8:1

Subject Index

103-104, 117, 120,
124-125, 133

Kempis, Thomas à, 50, 52, 54,
128
Kinesics ("body language"),
29
Kolbe, St. Maximilian, 116
Koontz, Sr. Linda, 89
Kossicki, Fr. George, 73, 105,
109, 130
Kowalska, Blessed Faustina,
7, 30, 49, 53, 60, 102-103,
126

Last rites (*see* Anointing of
the sick)
Latin Mass, 119-120
Laughter, 27
Liturgical year, pastoral care
and the, 110-113
Lourdes, 89
Luther, Martin, 120

MacNutt, Francis, 32, 90,
127, 131
Maronite rite, 120
Martin, Ralph, 61-62, 64, 99,
130, 131
Mary, 95, 110, 115, 123
Maternity, 83-85
McCall, Dr. Kenneth, 126
McKenna, Sr. Briege, 50, 128

Medicine and prayer, 12-13
Medjugorje, 89
Mother Teresa, 15, 17, 19, 36,
102, 132
Morrow, Lance, 130
Mount Athos, 107
Murray, Andrew, 39, 128

Neuhaus, Fr. John, 127
Nonverbal communication in
pastoral care, 24-33, 37

Old age, 77-78

Paralanguage, 26-29
Pastoral caregivers as
Christ's servants, 15-16
Pastoral care ministry, 3-5;
and holiness, 6-7
Patients, as caregivers, 5;
love for, 5-7, 14; personal
appearance, 25; problem-
atic, 21-22; reverence for,
14-15
Paul VI, 120
Pediatrics, 85-86
Pike, Kenneth, 21, 102, 127,
132
Pio, Fr., 126
Poyatos, Fernando, 132
Praise in the mass, 94-95
Prayer, 34-39, 93-117;
accepting God's will,